A to Z of Teaching in FE

Other Titles in the Essential FE Toolkit Series

Books for Lecturers

Teaching Adults – Amanda Hayes

Teaching the FE Curriculum – Mark Weyers

e-Learning in FE – John Whalley, Theresa Welch and Lee Williamson

FE Lecturer's Survival Guide – Angela Steward

FE Lecturer's Guide to Diversity and Inclusion – Anne-Marie Wright, Sue Colquhoun, Jane Speare and Tracey Partridge

How to Manage Stress in FE – Elizabeth Hartney

Guide to Teaching 14–19 – James Ogunleye

Ultimate FE Lecturer's Handbook – Ros Clow and Trevor Dawn

Getting the Buggers Motivated in FE – Susan Wallace

How to Teach in FE with a Hangover – Angela Steward

Books for Managers

Everything You Need To Know about FE Policy – Yvonne Hillier

Middle Management in FE – Ann Briggs

Managing Higher Education in Colleges – Gareth Parry, Anne Thompson and Penny Blackie

Survival Guide for College Managers and Leaders – David Collins

Guide to Leadership and Governance in FE – Adrian Perry

Guide to Financial Management in FE – Julian Gravatt

Guide to Race Equality in FE – Beulah Ainley

Ultimate FE Leadership and Management Handbook – Jill Jameson and Ian McNay

A to Z for Every Manager in FE – Susan Wallace and Jonathan Gravells

Guide to VET – Christopher Winch and Terry Hyland

A to Z of Teaching in FE

Angela Steward

continuum

Continuum International Publishing Group

The Tower Building   80 Maiden Lane, Suite 704
11 York Road   New York
SE1 7NX   NY 10038

www.continuumbooks.com

British Library Cataloguing-in-Publication Data
A catalogue record for this book is available from the British Library.

ISBN: 0 8264 9080 8 (paperback)
      978 08264 9080 3

Typeset by BookEns Ltd, Royston, Herts.
Printed and bound in Great Britain by
Athenaeum Press Ltd., Gateshead, Tyne & Wear

For my sisters, Christine, Theresa and Stella,
and my sister-in-law Brenda,
who helped me find my way through life.

Contents

Acknowledgements

Many thanks to Professor Vernon Trafford at Anglia Ruskin University, and Professor Rob Fiddy and all the staff in the HE Faculty at City College Norwich, who helped me navigate the pathways of FE teaching.

Series foreword

THE ESSENTIAL FE TOOLKIT SERIES

Jill Jameson

Series Editor

In the autumn of 1974, a young woman newly arrived from Africa landed in Devon to embark on a new life in England. Having travelled half way round the world, she still longed for sunny Zimbabwe. Not sure what career to follow, she took a part-time job teaching EFL to Finnish students. Enjoying this, she studied thereafter for a PGCE at the University of Nottingham in Ted Wragg's Education Department. After teaching in secondary schools, she returned to university in Cambridge, and, having graduated, took a job in ILEA in 1984 in adult education. She loved it: there was something about adult education that woke her up, made her feel fully alive, newly aware of all the lifelong learning journeys being followed by so many students and staff around her. The adult community centre she worked in was a joyful place for diverse multi-ethnic communities. Everyone was cared for, including 90-year-olds in wheelchairs, toddlers in the crêche, ESOL refugees, city accountants in business suits and university level graphic design students. In her eyes, the centre was an educational ideal, a remarkable place in which, gradually, everyone was helped to learn to be who they wanted to be. This was the Chequer Centre, Finsbury, EC1, the 'red house', as her daughter saw it, toddling in from the crêche. And so began the story of a long interest in further education that was to last for many years . . . why, if they did such good work for so many, were FE centres so under-funded and unrecognized, so under-appreciated?

It is with delight that, 32 years after the above story began, I write the Foreword to *The Essential FE Toolkit*, Continuum's new book series of 24 books on further education (FE) for teachers and college leaders. The idea is to provide a comprehensive guide to FE in a series of compact, readable books. The suite of 24 individual books are gathered together to provide the practitioner with an overall FE toolkit in specialist, fact-filled volumes designed to be easily accessible, written by experts with significant knowledge and experience in their individual fields. All of the authors have in-depth understanding of further education. But: *'Why is further education important? Why does it merit a whole series to be written about it?'* you may ask.

At the Association of Colleges Annual Conference in 2005, in a humorous speech to college principals, John Brennan said that, whereas in 1995 further education was a 'political backwater', by 2005 FE had become 'mainstream'. John recalled that, since 1995, there had been '36 separate Government or Government-sponsored reports or white papers specifically devoted to the post-16 sector'. In our recent regional research report (2006) for the Learning and Skills Development Agency, my co-author Yvonne Hillier and I noted that it was no longer 'raining policy' in FE, as we had described earlier (Hillier and Jameson, 2003): there is now a torrent of new initiatives. We thought, in 2003, that an umbrella would suffice to protect you. We'd now recommend buying a boat to navigate these choppy waters, as it looks as if John Brennan's 'mainstream' FE, combined with a tidal wave of government policies, will soon lead to a flood of new interest in the sector, rather than end anytime soon.

There are good reasons for all this government attention on further education. In 2004/05, student numbers in LSC-funded further education increased to 4.2m, total college income was around £6.1 billion, and the average college had an annual turnover of £15 million. Further education has rapidly increased in national significance regarding the need for ever-greater achievements in UK education and skills training for millions of learners, providing qualifications and workforce training to feed a UK national economy hungrily in competition with other OECD nations. The 120 recommendations of the Foster Review (2005) therefore in the main encourage colleges to focus their work on vocational skills, social inclusion and achieving academic progress. This series is here to consider all three of these areas and more.

The series is written for teaching practitioners, leaders and managers in the 572 FE/LSC-funded institutions in the UK, including FE colleges, adult education and sixth form institutions, prison education departments, training and workforce development units, local education authorities and community agencies. The series is also written for PGCE/Cert Ed/City & Guilds Initial and continuing professional development (CPD) teacher trainees in universities in the UK, USA, Canada, Australia, New Zealand and beyond. It will also be of interest to staff in the 600 Jobcentre Plus providers in the UK and to many private training organizations. All may find this series of use and interest in learning about FE educational practice in the 24 different areas of these specialist books from experts in the field.

Our use of this somewhat fuzzy term 'practitioners' includes staff in the FE/LSC-funded sector who engage in professional practice in governance, leadership, management, teaching, training, financial and administration services, student support services, ICT and MIS technical support, librarianship, learning resources, marketing, research and development, nursery and crêche services, community and business support, transport and estates management. It is also intended to include staff in a host of other FE services including work-related training, catering, outreach and specialist health, diagnostic additional learning support, pastoral and religious support for students. Updating staff in professional practice is critically important at a time of such continuing radical policy-driven change, and we are pleased to contribute to this nationally and internationally.

We are also privileged to have an exceptional range of authors writing for the series. Many of our series authors are renowned for their work in further education, having worked in the sector for 30 years or more. Some have received OBE or CBE honours, professorships, fellowships and awards for contributions they have made to further education. All have demonstrated a commitment to FE that makes their books come alive with a kind of wise guidance for the reader.

Sometimes this is tinged with world-weariness, sometimes with sympathy, humour or excitement. Sometimes the books are just plain clever or a fascinating read, to guide practitioners of the future who will read these works. Together, the books make up a considerable portfolio of assets for you to take with you through your journeys in further education. We hope the experience of reading the books will be interesting, instructive and pleasurable and that experience gained from them will last, renewed, for many seasons.

It has been wonderful to work with all of the authors and with Continuum's UK Education Publisher, Alexandra Webster, on this series. The exhilarating opportunity of developing such a comprehensive toolkit of books probably comes once in a lifetime, if at all. I am privileged to have had this rare opportunity, and I thank the publishers, authors and other contributors to the series for making these books come to life with their fantastic contributions to FE.

Dr Jill Jameson
Series Editor
March, 2006

Introduction

A to Z of Teaching in FE by Angela Steward

In 1935, Phyllis Pearsall (1906–96), an artist, the daughter of a Hungarian map-maker, became lost on her way to a party in London one evening, unable to find the address of the party on the Ordnance Survey map. This incident so affected Phyllis that she spent the next year mapping London's 23,000 streets to create a new A to Z street atlas of London. She successfully published this masterpiece of information design in 1936, creating her own publishing company to do so when every publisher turned it down. The atlas was a runaway success in sales and is still a world leader in map design (Pearsall, 1990; Design Council, 2006).

Building on Pearsall's history, we could reflect on the reasons why an A to Z information mapping concept for multi-faceted and obscure landscapes is so useful. Essentially, a simple A to Z alphabetical list enables the universal categorization of complex information into a basic and familiar structure, helping users to quickly and easily locate essential items and follow internal references to linked pages. So, for readers interested in teaching in the highly complex, diverse, constantly changing world of further education, this new information guide, Angela Steward's *A to Z of Teaching in FE* provides as essential and useful a manual to the intricacies of FE as the A to Zs of local cities are when we need to find new places. As Angela puts it, 'The *A to Z of Teaching in FE* aims to help you find your way around the unknown territory and ever-changing environment of the FE sector.'

The A to Z provides a vital, straightforward, accessible and sometimes humorous guide to the new policies, initiatives, official terminology, jargon and key imperatives facing FE lecturers. Angela has many years' experience of working in further education as a lecturer herself. She has also carried out extensive research with staff in the sector. She therefore brings the benefits of considerable expertise and in-depth knowledge about FE to this new A to Z, mapping the difficult terrain of teaching in FE in ways that both inspire us to learn more about the sector and help us when we're feeling a bit lost at the latest barrage of acronyms from the most recent policy initiatives. Not only that, but Angela manages to do this with a wonderful sensitivity and warmth towards the most important people in the sector – our students and staff.

At a time when the Foster Review (2005), the government White Paper on FE (2006) and the Quality Improvement Agency (QIA) are calling for widespread rapid improvements in teaching and learning across the FE sector, this book provides an excellent handbook on teaching in FE for lecturers and academic-related staff. If you feel you need to know more about FE from a straightforward, useful, helpful and light-hearted information source, this book is essential reading for you. I thoroughly recommend that you read it straight away!

Dr Jill Jameson
Director of Research

References

Pearsall, P. (1990) *From Bedsitter to Household Name: The personal story of the first 50 years of the Geographers' A–Z Map Company.* Sevenoaks, Kent: Geographers' A–Z Map Company.

Design Council (2006) *Phyllis Pearsall: Map Designer (1906–1996).* Article on Design Council website (accessed August 3rd, 2006) www.designmuseum.org/design/phyllis-pearsall.

Introduction

If you want to find your way around an unfamiliar city when on a visit to family or friends, on a business trip or as a tourist, a good idea is to consult an A to Z, which provides you with the exact location of your destination. You use the grids and references in the guide to find your way through unknown territory. The *A to Z of Teaching in FE* aims to help you find your way around the unknown territory and ever-changing environment of the FE sector. For a newcomer to teaching in FE, the A to Z provides quick and accessible entries explaining some of the current terminology used in teaching in FE and offers ideas for you to consider and think about and perhaps adopt in your own teaching sessions. If you have been working as a lecturer in a college for some time, you will have experienced the implementation of new policies, the escalation of fresh initiatives and the pressures of funding regimes and targets. All these factors have a bearing on the context in which lecturers teach, and when you are busy with the day-to-day demands of working in the FE sector it is a struggle to stay abreast of all the changes and keep up to date.

Like any profession, teaching in FE is full of terminology, jargon and acronyms which can be bewildering for lecturers. Trying to decode the jargon is often tricky, as when everyone else seems to know what is being talked about you may feel you don't like to ask. The entries put in plain words some of the specialist language and abbreviations which managers, teacher-educators and lecturers bandy about.

I draw on experiences from my own practice, and ideas shared by colleagues, and the entries contain comments and personal views on different aspects of teaching in FE. I acknowledge that the FE sector is diverse and what might be relevant for some lecturers may not be applicable for others. This A to Z offers a light-hearted, yet thought-provoking, approach to countless facets of teaching in FE and combines the opportunity to look up practical solutions rapidly as well as some of the theories underpinning teaching in FE.

A is for ...

Accelerated Learning – increasing the speed of learning. You may have often wondered why some students learn faster than others, or why some students are receptive to new ideas when others are not. The rationale for accelerated learning is that in a fast-changing world, and with employment presenting constant new challenges, making sense of an increasing volume of information rapidly is essential. The theory (Smith, 1996) is that you appeal to a student's full range of intelligences and learning preferences, take into account social and emotional influences in learning and get students to become aware of how they learn. Intelligence is not conceived of as a fixed or single quotient, but comprises difference intelligences which can be developed, and it makes sense to use students' strongest intelligences as they learn. If you only use lectures, textbooks and coursework, then it is considered that only those students strong in particular forms of intelligences will do well, and others will struggle. To absorb information rapidly it is suggested that you use a range of strategies, e.g. web-based learning and role-play, to encourage students to think logically and creatively. Whatever the theory, a variety of strategies and approaches to teaching and learning, and an awareness of their social and emotional needs, will create a positive learning environment for students. See **Multiple Intelligences** and **VAK** for more information.

Acronym – word formed from the initial letters of other words.
Every workplace is full of professional jargon including

acronyms, and the FE sector is no exception. An example is that the development agency for the sector has been known over the years as FEU, FEDA and LSDA, and now it is to be split and part of it known as LSN, i.e. the Learning and Skills Network. The other part is renamed QIA, that's the Quality and Improvement Agency for Lifelong Learning. It's no wonder that it's a job to keep up! The trouble with acronyms is that the person who uses them assumes that everyone else knows what they're talking about. Often you feel as if you're the only one who is in the dark and feel too embarrassed to admit you haven't a clue what they mean. Be brave and ask. You'll make someone's day when they can explain what the set of initials means!

Andragogy – used to describe the way adults learn, which under contrasts with the term pedagogy, used for the way children learn.

As the majority of students in further education colleges are adults, i.e. 19 years of age or over, this is an important concept for lecturers to consider. There is an assumption central to andragogy that adults learn differently from children. A word of caution here.

First, it is a mistake to think of adult learners as a homogenous group. It is argued that adults have accumulated experience which becomes a resource for learning, and that they exhibit a readiness and intrinsic motivation to learn. Yet adults bring diverse educational, cultural and life experiences to their college studies, which means they may be confident or anxious, organized or disorganized and more or less motivated. Adult students in FE may be completing the last year of a full-time degree course or may be accessing a language course as newly-arrived internationals. Adult students may be holding down responsible jobs, bringing up a family single-handedly, coping with unemployment, nursing elderly relatives, struggling with stroppy teenagers or confronting retirement. It is abundantly clear that the motivations and expectations of adults as students are extremely diverse.

Second, andragogy is distinguished by the notion that adult students are self-directed, i.e. know what they want to learn and how they want to learn it. However, there is an alternative argument which contends that when adults become students they tend to take on the characteristics of younger students and leave their responsible, adult selves outside the classroom (Hanson, 1996). I expect you have you experience of adult students who are needy, moody in class and miss assessments. Rather than assume that self-direction is an attribute that adult students bring with them at the start of a course, the FE lecturer's role is to support and encourage them to be self-directed as they progress through it. This can be done by gradually being less directive and negotiating more, helping adult students set their own goals, encouraging action planning, and explaining that knowledge and skills are gained through everyday experiences at home and/or work and not just from books or in college. It is the unknown or new experiences, e.g. just attending college or going on to a higher level course, that affect students and it is not denigrating students as adults to support them as learners just as you would younger students.

Assessment – involves making a judgement about the progress of a particular student's learning or their achievement.

As an FE lecturer you probably spend a lot of time thinking about formal assessment such as your students' final projects, tests or examinations, which are all summative assessments, i.e. taken at the end of their course of study. When you are planning a learning programme you check that you've covered all the specified learning outcomes to enable your students to gain a particular qualification or achieve the criteria set by an examination board or a vocational or professional awarding body. Generally, 'what counts' for students is achieving the formal qualification that may be a passport to a higher level course, a job opening or career opportunity. Of course, you also want your students to be successful and you have to keep in mind the final assessment when presenting the course content and gear your teaching to preparing students to achieve their qualifications.

The emphasis on the end product of your course may encourage students to consider anything that is not directly related to this as a waste of time. This narrow focus means students question the relevance of everything they do, which may lead them to underestimate the value of what they bring to the course from outside through their prior experiences and previous education and training. There is a tendency for students to sit passively and rely on you to supply the information that will get them their qualifications.

It is not just your students who focus on their final achievement. Your department – or area of provision – is accountable for its results, and the Learning and Skills Council (LSC), through the self-assessment process, monitors the targets set by your college for achievement. However, as Ofsted inspections now focus on teaching and learning and the experience of students, if you picture your teaching sessions as a pathway to summative assessment, not only do you prepare students for success in their formal assessment but you also make students aware of how individual activities contribute to the overall course requirements. You can start off with a diagnostic assessment to establish what students do and do not know. This encourages students to see the relevance of class activities to the required outcomes as they accumulate skills and knowledge. Next, class discussions, student queries and your questioning become opportunities for informal assessment. It soon becomes clear whether students have understood the knowledge or skills being studied, which enables you to adjust the pace of your sessions if necessary and thus demonstrate that you are aware of students' concerns. Checking students' learning throughout the course, i.e. formative assessment, provides you and your students with information about their progress, which is an important motivating force.

To maximize the effectiveness of students' learning, encourage students to think about how they learn and talk about not only the content of their learning programme but also how they respond to particular activities. Formative assessment involves discussing with students what their particular strengths or weaknesses are, why they succeeded or failed and how they felt about this, i.e. raising students' awareness of the way they learn and thus the means by which they can achieve. Formative assessment provides the student with continual feedback about how to improve their chances of success, involves them in their learning and encourages them to take responsibility for realizing it (Jones, 2005). This is not about identifying learning styles, but discussing with students what they need to do and understand in order to gain a particular level in the desired qualification, e.g. Pass, Grade A, Distinction, Fully Competent. Students need to be as familiar as you are with the set of criteria all candidates will need to meet in order to achieve success and the best tool you can give them is the ability to make a judgement about their own progress and assess their own achievement, rather than relying on you. Find out more about assessment in **Giving feedback**.

Attitudinal-based Learning

There is a body of opinion that suggests that if you focus on changing a student's attitude to their college work, i.e. the way they think about it, then this will have a positive effect on their learning (Dunn and Finnemore, 2004). This is based on the belief that a student's decision to learn is tempered by the perceived usefulness of the new skills or knowledge and how well they fit into the student's circumstances and situation, i.e. their personal and/or working environment. The student decides what is useful to learn and how it is to be used – or rejects it. You can teach all you like, but in the end it is the student who controls his or her learning. The job of the lecturer is to convince students that engaging in learning is a beneficial choice for them to make.

When you encounter students who are resistant to, or reject learning, you probably get frustrated and may ask yourself what makes them like this. Instead of standing in front of the class explaining why students should want to learn a particular topic you are teaching and telling them 'by the end of today's session you will achieve the following objectives ...' make connections with the students' current knowledge, e.g.

by reviewing previous sessions through question and answer, brainstorming what is already known, and demonstrating their skills. These activities make explicit to students what they know and/or can do.

Confronting students immediately with new knowledge or skills makes students frame questions such as: Do I need this information? Is it going to be useful to me? If students can make connections with what they know, i.e. what you have just made explicit to them through the introductory activities, then they will be less likely to reject the new material. The next step is to ask students to consider how this learning can be applied, e.g. to their workplace, to another session, in another context. In this way the students are ready to explore new ideas and work out the 'answers' using the information they have just re-examined. If you avoid challenging students' early 'answers' but supplement them and superimpose new material using a mix of delivery and activities, students gradually provide new ideas or thoughts themselves as they assimilate the new material. The knack is to provide students with information that fits into what they already know, and to do this you have to make that prior knowledge or skill explicit. In this way you can bring students to the conclusion that the new knowledge or skill is useful to them, whether it be academic, vocational or professional development. Students' attitude to learning will change when they can see its usefulness.

B is for ...

Behaviour

Let's deal with bad behaviour, as this is what many lecturers are concerned about.

It is only in recent years that discussions among lecturers about students' behaviour have become more frequent. If you teach in the FE sector then there is an expectation that students are, on the whole, self-disciplined. Often ways of behaving are modelled on what would be acceptable in a particular vocational area, and lecturers tend to admonish students for behaviour they consider would be unacceptable in the workplace, and insist on good work habits. As the student cohort in FE colleges has widened and the groups being taught have become more diverse and perhaps not affiliated to a workplace, so lecturers have experienced more variation in the way students behave.

The majority of students enrolled on FE courses are committed to their studies and work conscientiously. Nevertheless, you also encounter students who don't want to be there, who either struggle with the demands of their qualifications or aren't challenged by the level of work – or maybe get their rewards from anti-social behaviour rather than educational achievement. For a minority, it is easier to achieve status amongst one's peers by anti-social behaviour than through the discipline required to be successful on a college course. However, lecturers have an advantage as they are not usually seen as the 'enemy' by this group – unlike the police, probation service or prison authorities. Nonetheless, lecturers do represent a 'softer' authority, and have a role in promoting socially acceptable behaviour within the college.

Violent incidents are reported to be increasing, but for most lecturers they are rare. However, such incidents need to be dealt with on a college-wide basis and it is not advisable for individual lecturers to try to sort them out on their own. The safety of everyone is paramount, so get students away from the violent incident as quickly as possible, and then get help. If you experience violent behaviour in your class, or are aware of serious incidents involving students outside class, then you have a responsibility to report these to the college management.

What FE lecturers encounter more often is disruptive behaviour, e.g. shouting across the room, ignoring requests, laughing and joking at inappropriate times, arguing about the way things are done, chucking things about. Sometimes this behaviour is deliberate and designed to disrupt or be offensive. If you respond by saying how it affects *you* as a lecturer – rather than berating the student(s) – this usually takes the heat out of the moment. Saying something general along the lines of: 'I can't help anybody when there's such a racket', means that if the bad behaviour was deliberately meant to antagonize you or undermine you, then you have not risen to the bait. If you shout at students to make them behave, or threaten them, the response to such a 'telling-off' is likely to be cat-calling or whistling from group members. Nothing gives disruptive students more pleasure than to see you angry and uptight. Identify what triggers your anger – I know for me it is students mimicking me or another student – and make an effort to model the sort of behaviour you expect and stay calm.

If the bad behaviour was not malicious, e.g. the result of a joke gone too far, frustration or showing off, then saying how it affects you – more often than not – elicits some sort of apology. If this is not forthcoming, one tactic is to leave the room yourself – rather than send students out – and say, 'I'll give you five minutes to sort yourselves out and when I come back we'll carry on with the lesson.' This usually works, but if it doesn't don't carry on, don't teach, just sit silently at your desk or work-station. Don't discuss the disruptive incident, listen to excuses, accept justifications or dole out blame. Often silence is more effective in dealing with bad behaviour.

At the end of the allocated time, tell the students what your expectations are about their behaviour in college, what they are going to do in the next session and what they need to prepare or bring. In this way, you set the rules for your class and take control of the situation. In an ideal world, rules should be mutually agreed, but if there are no rules then students will form their own. Taking control in this way gives students a chance to change their behaviour and make a fresh start – if they don't respond, only then will you need to use your authority and start some sort of disciplinary procedure. Sometimes you have to exercise control and, temporarily, take on the role of disciplinarian with individual students so that they, and everyone else in the group, can achieve their educational aims.

Behaviourism – theory based on study of observed behaviour.
Behaviourist theories derived from the notion that behaviour should be observed just like the phenomena in all other natural sciences (Minton, 2005). Behaviourism concentrates on a person's behaviour, i.e. what can be observed. The key ideas include a stimulus (a task to be completed or skill to be learnt), a response (the student's response to the task) and reinforcement (positive or negative feedback from doing the activity – or from the lecturer – which shapes the student's success or otherwise in undertaking the task). These theories draw heavily on experiments with animals, such as rats and monkeys, and this is one aspect of behaviourism that nowadays leads to it being rejected as relevant to current notions of teaching and learning.

However, achieving competence in a vocational area draws strongly on behaviourist theories. It can be argued that this approach leaves no room for individuality or creativity in learning as the criteria for achievement are so tightly described, e.g. NVQ performance criteria. If lecturers keep in mind how they use their power to shape behaviour, and acknowledge that as assessors of NVQs they are acting on behalf of employers and awarding bodies, then behaviourist theories can be useful for developing skills, rewarding good study habits and highlighting good practice through feedback. See **Giving Feedback** for more information.

Boundaries

There is a tendency to think of defining boundaries just to set the limits to ways of behaving in your class and around college. Certainly, if you don't set and agree with students certain boundaries, then groups tend to set their own, which may be at odds with the wider college community. Students need to know how far they can go. For example, clear boundaries have to be set involving personal safety and mutual respect.

However, if you consider boundaries with regard to teaching and learning, they can be self-imposed by students and need to be challenged. You cannot assume students regard college in a positive light. Students come to your class with a particular view of their capability, and some may describe themselves as 'a failure', 'thick' or 'a bit slow'. In these descriptions, students place boundaries around themselves. Creating such a defensive boundary helps to mitigate the effects of failure for the individual, but limits them as they are wary of further learning experiences in case they face failure again. If students have previously had unsatisfactory learning experiences this does not mean that they are not capable. Perhaps a combination of factors – such as emotional upset, unsuitable teaching methods, personality clashes, lack of employment opportunity, family problems – may have drained their enthusiasm and motivation.

As a lecturer, it is important for you to help students dismantle boundaries they set up and give them the chance to modify their opinion of themselves by shaping positive learning experiences. A simple way of doing this is by accepting where the student is now, chatting to them about what they would like to get out of the course, and referring to these hopes when you introduce an activity, e.g. 'this should help if you want to become a receptionist', or 'this should help improve your design skills'. Responding in this way recognizes their needs and demonstrates your support for the student. Getting students to take risks – which may not seem risks at all to others – is also a way of enabling students to break out of their boundaries. Working with students they don't know, sharing ideas, presenting group feedback or giving a demonstration are all 'risks' and ways in which formerly negative students can engage in learning activities. Students can gradually let the self-imposed boundaries come down as they gain practical skills and knowledge. You can recognize when this is happening when you hear so-called disengaged students say something like: 'I got this off the internet, what do you think?'

Bullying – dominating others by threat or force.

Bullying is often difficult to spot as the perpetrators make sure that lecturers aren't around when it happens. Students are vulnerable to bullies as they come and go from college, or during breaks between sessions. Bullies often start by bullying for items they have forgotten to bring to college, or for homework or coursework they haven't done. If they are successful, the targets can become more frequent and bigger until they are bullying for mobile phones, iPods, money, mountain bikes, etc. and threatening physical violence. A dilemma for lecturers is whether they aggravate the situation when they deal with it. If a student confides in you that they have been bullied, do you keep the confidence of the student or reveal the incident? If the bullying happens outside college, what is your position? These are difficult questions, and the answers aren't easy. You have to send out the moral message that bullying in any form is not acceptable. Bullying humiliates and ridicules the victim, and undermines their self-esteem. Take action. Report incidents of bullying. Support victims: offer protection and provide advice.

C is for . . .

Concept Building – developing thoughts and ideas.
Although this sounds complicated, it really isn't. Here are
some simple steps. First, get students to list ideas/informa-
tion/thoughts regarding a specific problem or question. Then
ask them to group the items appropriately by ranking them,
putting them in sequence, or matching them, i.e. sorting into
whatever goes together. When this is done, question students
about why they have done it this way, then get them to think
about a label, i.e. a name or category, for each group. Now get
them to compare and contrast the labels and draw out –
through explanation, questioning and analysis – what con-
nects the different labels. Ask them if they can put this into
one word, or perhaps two. This word or phrase is the concept
you are striving to elicit! The activity goes from concrete
experience to abstract conceptualization – easy or what! Post-
it notes are brilliant for this activity. Get more information in
Kolb's Learning Cycle.

Constructivism – a theory about how people learn.
Constructivism is a theory about how people learn which
basically says that people construct their own understanding
and knowledge of the world through experiencing things and
reflecting on those experiences (Hoban, 2002). When we
encounter something new we have to reconcile it with our
previous ideas and experiences. We may change what we
believe, or discard new information as irrelevant. In any case,
we are active creators of our own knowledge. To do this we
must ask questions, explore and assess what we know.

In the classroom or workshop, constructivism can point towards a number of different ways of teaching and learning. It usually means encouraging students to use active techniques, e.g. real-world problem-solving and inquiry-based learning, to create more knowledge and then to reflect on and talk about what they are doing and how their understanding is changing. The lecturer guides the activity to address pre-existing knowledge and then students build on it. You can appreciate why the theory has the name it has! Constructivism is an alternative to behaviourist theories as the theory behind constructivism is that people differ from each other in their construction of events, despite social processes and cultural similarities.

Critics of constructivism imply that although it explains how personal knowledge construction occurs, it does not explain how identity is constructed and how social interactions influence an individual's learning, although one important variation of constructivism, 'social constructivism', deals specifically with collaborative learning between people (Vygotsky, 1962, 1978). An important question the critics raise is how an individual learns completely new knowledge, i.e. you can't build on what you don't know! As we're not dealing with rocket science in FE perhaps that's irrelevant – but the contribution of the social context of learning is certainly relevant to consider, as a number of social constructivists have done (Vygotsky, 1962, 1978; Bruner, 1986, 1990). See also Zone of Proximal Development.

Cooperative Learning – working collaboratively.

It is important that cooperative learning tasks should be ones for which group participation is a genuine asset for everyone in the group (Jacques, 2000). Some tasks are more effectively done by individuals acting alone, e.g. gathering information and reading it. Tasks that are suitable for cooperative learning involve design projects and problem-solving, where there is more than one way of arriving at a solution, or working together to create a worthwhile product. Tasks should also offer a challenge to all students – particularly in mixed groups – and afford students an opportunity to make different kinds of contributions by demanding a variety of abilities and skills.

Creativity

To be considered creative, a thought or product must be novel or original to the person who creates it. Creativity in teaching and learning is not just used to describe the production of original objects such as a picture, a poem or a new pattern or design. Neither does it focus on describing the characteristics of individuals who produce such work. In teaching and learning in FE, creativity is applied to new interpretations of materials or knowledge through the process of critical thinking and using imagination. Creativity in this sense brings together both the person and the product. What you already know as a lecturer may be new to your students, and so you need to provide opportunities for students to actively engage with new materials, skills or course content to create their own understanding of it. It is through thinking about alternative ways of doing things, or imagining different ways of seeing things, that students create new knowledge. Creativity is demonstrated when students go beyond their existing ways of thinking and remark, 'I never thought of it like that before', or say something like, 'Now I know that, I'll think about it differently.'

Immersion in creative experiences is central to courses in, say, Art and Design, Photography and Fashion. However, lecturers teaching other subjects can also adopt inventive strategies and use more ingenious resources. Good ways of encouraging students to be creative in their thinking are brainstorming, drawing scenarios instead of discussing them, role-playing problems, visualization exercises, swapping/changing roles and conducting imaginary interviews. Rather than just telling students something, i.e. transferring new knowledge, instead try to develop strategies that support the students' own creation of new knowledge.

Curriculum – a course of study.
The origin of the word curriculum is interesting. It is the Latin word for a course – but not the course of study that we relate it to now. The course was the stadium for chariot races in Roman times. It sometimes seems that coping with curriculum change is as precarious and challenging as a chariot race! Well, perhaps not quite as challenging! Nevertheless, curriculum change raises important issues for FE lecturers.

One way of thinking about the curriculum is as the published plans for what has to be covered or included in a course of study. Who decides what is to be covered in the curriculum? The Learning and Skills Council (LSC) is charged with producing a flexible curriculum for post-16 learning. The Qualifications and Curriculum Authority (QCA) develops pre-16 curriculum, and in 2005 plans were set out in the government's White Paper *14–19 Education and Skills* for transforming the curriculum for that age range, which will ultimately affect colleges. Currently, the QCA monitors qualifications in colleges and at work – and more and more it is employers who decide what is relevant and important curriculum content. Any attempts by policy makers at significant curriculum change will have an impact on teaching and learning in your college.

In England there has been a longstanding divide between a vocational and academic curriculum. Despite numerous government White Papers, the education and training curriculum was perhaps more suited to previous times than to the twenty-first century. Curriculum 2000 is intended to allow students a more flexible curriculum, as it is possible to combine vocational and academic subjects. Schools are allowed to drop the statutory National Curriculum requirements at Key Stage 4, so that pupils can follow a more work-related curriculum. Although both these curriculum initiatives are based on the existing qualifications framework, Key Skills have been incorporated as part of the curriculum. The reasoning behind this is that a set of generic skills is thought to be required in the workplace and should be developed both within education and employment. These initiatives arise from the notion that students should have the opportunity to develop a range of skills which prepare them for the future, rather than just the skills for a specific job, which could become redundant. Previously, the curriculum had been based solely on subjects and this radical widening was part of a package intended to make it more attractive to less academic students.

The traditional view that the purpose of the curriculum is to transmit a body of knowledge from one generation to the next is being replaced by a curriculum for developing a skilled workforce in a more uncertain world. Lifelong learning is central to new curriculum initiatives, and students are exhorted to continue in education until the age of 18 and to learn throughout life. Lifelong learning is not necessarily promoted for individual empowerment, but to enable individuals to cope with the adjustments necessary to survive in a rapidly changing workplace and changing society in general. Behind every curriculum initiative sits assumptions about the purpose of education in a modern society.

If curriculum changes are mandatory, you do not have much flexibility in implementation. However, determining your own course programme, schedule or scheme of work requires exercising your professional judgement. It is recognized that the quality of students' learning is linked to the quality of lecturers' learning. Implementing a new curriculum forces lecturers to question existing ways of teaching and learning, and provides a purpose for lecturers' learning. Consequently, some of the most effective learning for lecturers is through tackling the complexity of curriculum development projects and generating new ways of approaching their subject. The choices you make to implement the curriculum, e.g. sequencing the content, developing new teaching–learning strategies, designing new assessments and devising standards for evaluation, enable you to articulate your own beliefs about the purpose and nature of education and training in the FE sector, and transform highly prescriptive and standardized curriculum content into stimulating courses of study which support students' learning. Read more about curriculum implementation in **Planning Programmes**. For more information about generic skills, look under **Key Skills**.

D is for . . .

Deep Learning – learning that is meaningful.
The theoretical framework of approaches to learning termed 'deep' and 'surface' was developed through research with university students (Marton and Saljo, 1997) However, the framework is a useful way of considering the approach FE students take to learning, whatever their level of study. Deep learning is a term coined to describe learning that enables students to understand and apply knowledge. This is contrasted with surface learning, which is just trying to reproduce what has been presented or transmitted by memorizing it.

Surface learning has a place in any subject, e.g. being able to label basic components, spell specialist terms, perform simple skills, remember important dates and names, etc. Although surface learning enables students to recall and recite information and reproduce it in tests, quizzes or exams, it does not help students fully understand a subject, or see its relevance to other aspects of their curriculum. The way students learn is affected by their perception of what they have to do in order to achieve. Therefore, if you set numerous tests or activities requiring recall, that is the sort of learning you will encourage. This may be a relevant and satisfactory outcome for some introductory qualifications, those at entry level or as a knowledge base from which to build. In such a situation, testing development of 'confidence' where there is no absolute standard can be done through comparison with a student's own previous achievement. This approach is called self-referenced assessment, and is ideal for students who may only be able to achieve very small steps when judged by conventional standards or tests.

However, if you want students to develop their ideas, relate new ideas to previous knowledge, make sense of what has been learned and apply their new knowledge and skills to different contexts, i.e. engage in deep learning, then not only must these elements be incorporated into the assessment criteria but also encouraged in teaching and learning strategies used throughout the course. It is your choice of particular teaching and assessment strategies that nurtures deep learning. The lecturer's role is to employ a variety of teaching methods and prepare students for independent learning by incorporating study skills – relevant to the level of study – into sessions to raise students' awareness of ways they can be responsible for their own learning and success.

Trying to cover too much content in a short time, which results in a heavy workload for students, does not allow for time to work at topics in depth. In contrast, if you allow students to make choices, e.g. pick their own project/assignment and then support them in planning it, then a deep approach to learning is more likely as the work is meaningful to the students and they are self-motivated. Students' self-motivation is important but lecturers can motivate students too. Your encouragement will sustain students' motivation and your support will help them to persevere and stick with their studies.

A key way to promote deep learning is getting students to do the work rather than you doing it for them, e.g. researching material and sharing it on an intranet, summarizing information, interpreting graphs, preparing demonstrations or getting facts and figures from the internet. If students are engaged in the activity with others, say in groups of two or three, they are more likely to make connections with their previous learning and the new concepts being investigated, as they discuss ideas with other students. By collaborating with their peers and sharing information, students begin to understand and make sense of new material.

Deep learning doesn't just happen, though. Students need a well-structured knowledge base to start from. If you follow-up tutor-led presentations with opportunities for questions, discussion sessions or student-led seminars, you provide an opportunity for students to modify their learning, change their ideas and deepen their knowledge base. Involving students in their learning and devising problem-based tasks and assessments are other opportunities you can provide for students to engage in deep learning. Fostering reflection as part of tackling problems also encourages deep learning, as students develop their skills of evaluation and analysis. You can then turn the tables on students and get them to use these skills to judge whether their work is adequate and sufficient, rather than respond to questions from them such as 'Have I done enough?' or 'Is it all right?' With your support, and through purposeful discussion, students will be able to decide for themselves whether their work requires modification, ie you are encouraging them to take responsibility for their own learning through learning that is meaningful. More about deep learning is to be found in **Solo Taxonomy**.

Demonstration – a method of instruction by showing others how to do something.

Demonstrations are an excellent teaching method for lecturers to use, particularly if students are trying to acquire skills, set up their own experiments or tackle a creative project. But it is not as easy as it looks! There is a big difference between you doing something as an expert and then expecting your students to be able to demonstrate the skill themselves. If you ever watch TV quiz shows you'll know what I mean. The contestants watch an expert demonstrate a skill and they have to try to do the same thing immediately. They end up splattered in paint, covered in flour and chocolate or with everything in bits and pieces, much to everyone's amusement – and to top it all, their end product usually bears little resemblance to the expertly made one!

Although learning from mistakes can be fun, and we have to reassure students that mistakes may be inevitable at first there are some simple steps a lecturer can take to avoid real chaos. Depending on the skill, and if it is possible, it is a good idea to demonstrate it at 'normal' speed first and then repeat it more slowly while giving a running commentary.

The commentary draws students' attention to the complexity of the skill and makes them aware of the really tricky bits. To help students when they have a go themselves it is a good idea to put step-by-step reminders on a whiteboard or flip chart so students can quickly check the next step without calling out to you or needing your help – remember you can only be in one place at one time.

If the demonstration is going to take a longish time, e.g. preparing a chicken for roasting, changing a car wheel, throwing a pot, then make sure all students can clearly see what you are doing and hear what you are saying. A student could then be asked to try out the skill, and you and the group could prompt them and support them if needed. Another idea is to video the demonstration so that students can access the information later if they wish. Like any other teaching method, demonstrations require planning: gathering the resources, ensuring safety, providing appropriate protective clothing and checking the time it will take.

DFES – the Department for Education and Skills.
This department is responsible for the government's education and skills strategy and policy and accountable for public money allocated for this purpose by parliament. The ministerial team is headed by a Secretary of State for Education, and there is a minister with responsibility for the FE sector. Currently the Minister of State for HE and Lifelong Learning has responsibility for all post-19 policy and for bringing coherence to HE, FE, adult skills, the LSC and lifelong learning agenda. The website (www.dfes.gov.uk) is a source of current news and up-to-date information about education policy and reform and you can access publications or order them online.

Didactic – instruction as a way of teaching.
Didactic is now a 'dirty' word with Ofsted inspectors, so it's best if you know what it means! Although it just means using instruction techniques to teach, what inspectors don't like is

the tendency of lecturers who regard themselves as instructors to lay down the law, be too directive and give orders to students. Nowadays, training in vocational education does not have to be just about telling – or shouting - instructions and taking charge of trainees by belittling them. These activities have no place in a college nowadays.

Disability

The Disability Discrimination Act (1995) was fully implemented in 2004. The time between the Act being passed and implemented was to allow for the allocation of capital expenditure required and for works to be carried out. Alterations were made to colleges to enable access to buildings and provide appropriate accommodation and learning resources. Finance needed to be found for the provision of suitably qualified staff to support students with learning difficulties and disabilities. Assessing a student's needs involves being sensitive to a range of disabilities such as hearing loss, visual impairment, mobility issues or dyslexia, which may require specialist support or equipment. The assessment is to ascertain what will promote a student's independence – not to create dependency on you or others. It is meant to discover what is required so that students with disabilities can access learning effectively. For the lecturer, this means responding to individual student's requirements, considering their particular learning needs in your sessions and creating an inclusive environment. If you use specialist equipment in your teaching and learning sessions you will need to make regular audits to assess its suitability as well as auditing the classroom layout and other learning resources. You will need to liaise with colleagues who have the specialist skills and knowledge to guide you, and who will ensure that students are not having problems, being discriminated against or being victimized by college bureaucracy.

E is for . . .

Emotional Intelligence – the ability to manage one's own and other people's feelings.

The bad news is that success in life does not necessarily relate to a person's earlier success in college. Academic achievement does not predict later success in life, as people who start out with the same qualifications are not equally successful. After taking into account social class and chance, Goleman (1995, 1998) attributes this to emotional intelligence. His research revealed that those who are least successful in life lack social and emotional skills. It seems that being able to handle emotions – both in oneself and others – is critical to success in life. Lecturers in Management and Business Studies will be familiar with the notion of emotional intelligence as it applies to the corporate context. However, the relevance of this concept to FE lecturers is that – according to these research findings – for those unable to control their emotions, their intellectual capacity seems to be impaired. This is important to bear in mind for lecturers involved in students' vocational or academic education as an individual's inability to study effectively is discouraging – both for lecturers trying to raise achievement as well as for the student wanting to do well.

The good news is that Goleman reassures us that emotional intelligence can be improved or developed. You can learn to control and channel your emotions. There are two main ways of addressing issues of emotional intelligence with students. The first is to recognize that students are all very different in the way they react to teaching and learning and how they handle success, failure, and the challenge is of college work and regular attendance. Second, self-awareness of emotional intelligence can be raised with students – most appropriately in tutorials – and ways of handling emotions, e.g. anxiety about coursework, stress over deadlines and frustration at low grades, can be discussed. Talking about emotional issues is an important aspect of teaching and learning as, if students can control and channel their emotions effectively in the short term, they can give more attention to their college work.

As students come to realize that there are alternatives to reacting to disappointment and problems with an immediate burst of anger, desperation or hopelessness, and as they gradually face up to these emotions and discuss more reasonable ways of dealing with them, then there is a likelihood of developing social skills and the emotional intelligence that will increase their chances of success in the long term. There is a difference between occasional emotional outbursts in response to an identifiable crisis with college work or a student's personal life, and more prolonged displays of out-of-place emotional response. If students do not respond to talking about emotional issues in tutorials, and emotional issues continue to affect their college work, then it would be wise to seek help from a college counsellor or senior tutor both for your, and the student's, well-being.

Educational Connoisseurship

Eisner (1991) coined this term, which he defined as the ability to help others learn to see what they might otherwise not notice. A 'connoisseur' is someone who has specialist knowledge of a subject or is an authority in a particular area. A particular quality of a connoisseur is the ability to discriminate, e.g. they can distinguish between a genuine antique and a fake, make a distinction between an original artwork and a reproduction, and tell a quality product apart from an inferior one. Perhaps many of you will be aware of the latter which may, for instance, demand trying many different brands and types of wine in order to find one you really like! This requires the experience and ability to see and appreciate

– not merely look at (or taste!) – in order to know something about the item (or whatever) under scrutiny.

When Eisner applied this concept to educational settings, he envisaged the lecturer as an enthusiastic professional who is knowledgeable in their subject, and envisaged their role as helping students to 'see' and appreciate, and make judgements themselves. Educational connoisseurship has particular resonance for lecturers whose subjects involve students developing an expertise in designing, creating or performing. In creative arts this means freeing students from our own preconceptions and placing the student's experience at the centre of study. Creative practices shift and vary over time, and helping students develop educational connoisseurship encourages them to make personal evaluations of their work rather than rely on the judgements of lecturers and assessors, ie develop aesthetic intelligence.

e-Learning

The explosion of online technologies over the last ten years or so has created new possibilities for teaching and learning that should not be ignored. I am not suggesting that all learning should be e-learning, but it is evident that internet technologies can help establish conditions for learning by providing flexibility as to when and where learning can occur, e.g. overcoming problems of geographical isolation and time constraints, as well as creating new opportunities. Many colleges have pioneered e-learning and lecturers working in cutting edge environments will need no advice about developing curriculum. If you have not dipped your toe in the water yet, so to speak, then find more information in **New Technology**, and on two websites that offer up-do-date advice and loads of ideas specifically directed at the FE sector: www.ferl.becta.org.uk and www.jisc.ac.uk.

Encouragement

If there is one thing that singles out a 'good' lecturer in my book, it is giving encouragement to students. Some would say that there should be an entry for 'enthusiasm' rather than 'encouragement', as being enthusiastic about your subject is vitally important. For me, a problem with concentrating primarily on enthusiasm is that it focuses on a lecturer's teaching, whereas encouragement focuses on supporting students' learning. Of course, your enthusiasm for your subject is important, but if you really espouse student autonomy and self-directed learning, then everything you can do to support this is vital.

Encouragement helps students continue with their studies and keep going when things conspire against them. Time for study may disappear as crises arise at work. Emergencies at home send plans for writing assignments awry, as personal problems and deadlines come together and college work loses out. Supporting a student through situations such as these and encouraging them when they fall behind or lose confidence makes a difference. For students 'at risk' it is crucial. It may mean students keep up with your course, make progress and carry on with their qualification rather than give it all up and fail. It is your encouragement that makes a difference. Even when students are doing well, encouragement helps them strive more, stretch themselves, aim higher and perhaps gain better grades. Whatever their level, type of course or disposition, students respond to encouragement if it is given genuinely.

Equality

Equality is espoused by lecturers in theory, but is it promoted in practice? Do you treat all your students the same? When a colleague gave someone attention for a learning difficulty, some students accused him of depriving other students in the group from developing their potential. When I organized a class into groups for tutorial work, the last of the groups I met with felt they had been treated unfairly and that I had shown favouritism to the initial group in meeting them first. I expect both of us thought our actions were reasonable in the circumstances, but equality is also about the perceptions of others.

Students complaining about favouritism and being treated unfairly may be dismissed by many as childish or immature – but equality means respecting the rights of everyone to study. Equality is clearly an issue that concerns all lecturers and the more you think about it the more complex it becomes.

The issue centres on prejudice against people. These prejudices can be about gender, race, ethnicity, sexual orientation, disability, age, colour, religion or belief. When expressed in these terms, lecturers would say they don't respond differently to people in these categories. However, does your college discriminate against people by not accepting students for courses because they have a particular idea about a student's appearance, e.g. for hairdressing or management training? Does your college management ensure that marginalized students can fulfil their right to attend college without fear or harassment? Does a lecturer face disciplinary action for chauvinistic and discriminatory attitudes when dealing with students? Does sexual orientation become an issue discussed when assessing a student's progress? Do newly arrived internationals have access to language development? An FE college has a responsibility to promote equality of opportunity.

A role for lecturers is to raise understanding of how inequality and discrimination has a profoundly negative impact on people's lives, and stress to students that everyone has the right to equality of opportunity and regard. You can promote equality through your behaviour in the classroom, e.g. encouraging participation, accepting differences, and being open and impartial when responding to students. You must tackle incidents of intolerance and narrow-mindedness and not accept them. Being insular and bigoted has no place anywhere – but particularly not in an educational establishment. You can make it clear to students that you expect everyone to show respect for others, irrespective of their ethnicity, culture or religious background. The participation of marginalized and minority groups does not diminish but strengthens the college community. The responsibility of the college is to provide equal treatment and opportunities for all. How we do this fairly and without favouritism is a matter for open and ongoing discussion.

F is for ...

Facilitator – someone who helps promote learning.
You couldn't have an A to Z of FE teaching without including this section. Although your official title is 'lecturer' and you are employed as a 'teacher', the role you are expected to fulfil nowadays is that of a 'facilitator'. If you look at what the definition of facilitate is (i.e. make easy; promote; help forward), it places the role very firmly in the business of supporting students' learning. So, although some of you may not be too keen on being called a facilitator – and prefer the terms lecturer or teacher – you surely must agree that facilitating benefits students. After all, isn't that why you're in FE? Perhaps you might not be so averse to this title in the future now you know what it means. For further information, see **Teaching Styles**.

Formal Presentations – a method of teaching large groups.
Formal presentations can be lecturer-led or student-led. In this section I deal with lecturer-led presentations. Formal lecturer-led presentations are perceived by many students as a more adult way of learning. Students often comment that they like lecturer-led sessions in college as they make it feel different to school and they feel like 'proper' students. The term 'formal presentation' is nowadays used to describe a method of teaching either a large group of students in a lecture theatre, or a whole group in a class or workshop setting. The term 'lecture'

tends to be avoided, and is seldom used in FE as it is not perceived as student-friendly – but I think it can be.

If you are dealing with a large number of students there is a need for some formality so that the session can be organized for everyone's benefit. This does not necessarily mean that students cannot be actively involved in a lecturer-led session. A good 'presenter' can use a range of activities to engage students. However, you have to adapt your usual skills and techniques when dealing with a large group. The lecturer can still ask questions – but rather than ask for verbal responses, can give students time to think about the answers and respond in some other way. An example would be that the lecturer displays multiple-choice questions on a overhead projector or PowerPoint screen and ask students to jot down a, b or c, etc. This avoids the situation where part of the student group finds it difficult to hear a student response, or only very confident students respond and others switch off. Another way of engaging students is to ask them to think about what the next step might be in a process you are explaining and write it down. Alternatively, you can invite them to study a diagram or model of a theory you have introduced earlier and to identify important elements by looking at the numbers 1–5 on the diagram projected and jotting down the correct label or concept for each number. After that, reveal the completed diagram.

You can see how easy it is to involve everyone and how simple it is for students to check their answer. You could ask students to hazard a guess about a difficult concept. The following examples worked for me. Which of the two images is correct? Is it likely to be 50 per cent or 75 per cent? What problem is the graph revealing? What is the missing word in the chart? Perhaps you can think of examples that might work for your subject. As long as you give students time to think and jot down their response before you reveal the answer, they can be actively involved. Leadership of a large group in this way is preferable to asking students to stop talking so others can hear or losing their interest as you deliver a monologue.

If there is a lot of content to cover, ensure that you break it down into manageable 'chunks'. Students soon switch off if you keep talking for too long. Try and observe what the average concentration span is for the particular cohorts of students you teach. It is surprisingly short – even for the most dedicated student keen to get a much-needed qualification. Concentration may be as short as five minutes or may stretch to 20 minutes. After an appropriate time, get students to summarize the main points your presentation has covered so far. Only when they have written their points down do you reveal your own summary in bullet points. Students enjoy seeing how well their points match up. This activity keeps students interested and involved, and they may even start to challenge you and accuse you of missing something out – usually when you've had a little digression! All this adds to the fun and spontaneity of the presentation but, importantly, still keeps the focus on the topic.

It is important to follow up large-group presentations with some small-group work. Split your group into four 'teams' and allocate different tasks for the next session, e.g. one team write a seminar paper; one team research a new topic to share with whole group; and one team prepare a student-led presentation on a specific topic or practise a specific skill. You will be able to think of ideas that work for your students and your subject. While these three teams are working independently, you can see the other students for a group tutorial. Working with a smaller group makes interaction easier, you are able to get to know each other and it is an opportunity for reluctant students to contribute in a safer environment. In a smaller group, you can informally assess individual students' progress and provide support.

Perhaps you cannot deal with large groups as informally as you would wish, but you don't need to use formal presentations for every session. Sequence them every three or four sessions and interchange them with tutorials, seminars, student-led presentations and skills workshops. Formal, lecturer-led presentations are good for passing on technical information, introducing fundamental concepts, providing background information or sharing your expertise. Presentations can be really effective if you follow up with small-group work. If you break down long presentations by incorporating a variety of whole group activities that engage students, you can deal with their different concentration spans, motivations and abilities. Whatever you do, some students won't be completely happy, so address this by setting aside time at the end of the formal presentation for any pressing questions individuals may have and deal with them as the other students are packing away. You see, formal presentations can meet students' needs after all – but just don't call them 'lectures' on your session plan!

Foster – author of a report reviewing the FE sector in England.

It may seem strange to find someone's surname listed here. This name will become familiar across the FE sector as the impact of Sir Andrew Foster's review of the future role of FE, published in November 2005, is felt across the sector (Foster, 2005). It is bound to have an impact, as Foster calls for significant change and for the FE sector to put its house in order!

Foster's key recommendation is that the focus of colleges should be on the provision of skills and ensuring employability for students. Although the report says that academic courses, professional development courses and courses that contribute to social inclusion will not be excluded, it is pretty obvious that there will be some change in the level of provision in these areas. The report criticized the plethora of organizations in the sector charged with inspection, improvement and regulatory functions. Hear! Hear! I can hear you cheering. Foster favours a more streamlined LSC, with greater clarification of roles both nationally and regionally. He reports that management systems need to be put on a sound basis and gives no guarantees about improving funding or pay. Boo! Boo! One recommendation that has received a lot of media attention is that the 16 colleges (out of around 400 in England) classed as 'failing' would be given one year to shape up and develop before competition is introduced. Foster was invited by the DfES and the LSC to carry out an independent review and the government's response is published in a White Paper on FE Reform, Spring 2006. Foster's name will be on the lips of lecturers for many years to come.

Foundation Degrees

The Higher Education sector is undergoing a process of radical reform and investment. The government's target is that by 2010 50 per cent of 18 to 30-year-olds will have experienced higher education, which represents a huge increase in student numbers. Much of this higher education experience will take place in an FE setting, where students will study for Foundation degrees rather than conventional degrees offered by universities. Foundation degrees provide a crucial link in the progression route for those seeking qualifications for jobs such as high-level technician and associate professional. Foundation degrees are intended not only to meet the needs of the economy and employers, but also the demands from students themselves in the style of their delivery. They are vocationally based and work-focused, and offer flexible provision through part-time study and accessibility through attendance at local colleges. Foundation degrees appear in the Framework for Higher Educational Qualifications Levels at Level I (Intermediate), but can be topped up to a Bachelors degree with added study at Level H (Honours). For up-to-date information, access www.qca.org.uk.

Functional Skills – the new 3Rs

Did you know the 3Rs are now EMICT? Does that make sense to you? Does someone need help with their spelling? Functional skills, which are described as the new 3Rs, are the skills it is deemed every young person needs. Achieving mastery of the basics, identified in Functional Skills, is considered a pre-requisite for work and life. As colleges enrol more and more young people between 14 and 16, lecturers need to be familiar with what they are.

The core elements of Functional Skills are English, Maths and ICT (EMICT). These provide young people with essential knowledge, skills and understanding to enable them to 'function' confidently, effectively and independently in life and at work. English includes speaking, listening, reading, writing and being able to communicate effectively. Maths includes a range of concepts used to solve practical mathematical problems. In ICT, young people will need to demonstrate competence and confidence using technology to meet a variety of everyday situations.

The rationale for their introduction is that the possession of Functional Skills enables young people to participate and proceed in education, training and employment – as well as develop aptitudes, attitudes and behaviours that will enable them to make a positive contribution to the communities in which they live and work.

G is for ...

Gaining Access – exercising the right to education.

For most lecturers, their first thought when considering how students gain access to college courses is of ramps and lifts for those with a physical disability. Thankfully, these facilities now have to be provided by law and are at last in place. Physical access to college, although vital and important, is only one facet of gaining access. If you work in an FE college you probably don't think of it as a daunting place to enter. Yet for many students gaining access to courses is more than just getting to their class.

The location of a college, perhaps in the middle of town, may be fine for those gaining access by public transport but difficult for those who want to park their vehicle, e.g. those from outlying or rural areas who rely on their own transport. Conversely, if the college is out of town, how easy is it to gain access by public transport – not just at 9 o'clock in the morning, but in the evening when many students attend classes? Is public transport just as good at 9 o'clock at night? You may plan high-quality courses but if they are run at times when potential students are at work, taking children to school or fearful of going out at night, then the students you target cannot gain access to them.

Have you ever considered taking your course to your students, rather than expecting them to come to you? Many colleges run successful ventures in community halls and local venues. If childcare is a real issue for students, and perhaps the college crèche is too expensive, why not run a course in a venue where young children can enjoy supervised play while the adults are learning? Conversely, you could think about whether students need to attend college for every session or whether they could be learning at home. Flexibility of attendance may encourage people with commitments to consider enrolling on a course when part of it can be completed through home study using resources provided by the college.

Weekend workshops or one-day courses might appeal to those who are employed or have childcare responsibilities during the week. Running short courses may help students gain access to a new subject or activity, whereas they might not be confident enough to enrol on a longer programme. Enrolling on an introductory course requiring attendance, say, every Monday evening for four or six weeks may be an appealing way for potential students to gain access to college. Enrolling for just a few weeks doesn't seem such a commitment for students who lack the confidence or cash to attend a year-long course. Short bursts of successful experiences in college may be just the encouragement students need to confidently gain access to further courses.

As well as location, length and timing, do you have all the necessary resources to run a new course successfully? Have you ever been urged to run something new without a proper budget? When this is done, lack of appropriate resources means students cannot gain access to the skills or knowledge they are entitled to. Most colleges nowadays provide additional learning support, e.g. for literacy and numeracy development, dyslexia and language development. While this is invaluable, have you considered that your own use of language, or your own method of presentation to students may inhibit them gaining access to your teaching? Just because a student is sitting in front of you in class doesn't mean they are gaining access to learning. You have to take into account whether they can see, hear, understand and feel included.

The cost of courses, resources and transport often prevents potential students gaining access to college. An Education Maintenance Allowance (EMA) is available to help with everyday costs for those staying on at school after 16 or going to college, e.g. fares, books or equipment. The allowance depends on household income but could make a difference between a young person leaving education and gaining access to an FE college. Most colleges have excellent Information Centres where students can receive advice about gaining access to public funding, e.g. your college may be participating in the scheme for proving funding for over-19s through Adult Learning Grants, or funding from educational sponsors such as local businesses or charities. For more information, look under **Xtra support**.

Gender – sexual category.

College advertising material is full of photographs of happy, smiling students. Posters, information leaflets and brochures portray students in very mixed groups in terms of age, ethnicity and gender. When you look at students in college in workshops and classrooms, the picture is very different in several areas. Salons are full of females training to be hairdressers, whereas motor-vehicle workshops are full of males training to be mechanics. Classes in childcare or early years rarely have males in them. Gender issues are apparent. Are we being naïve when we accept that these vocational classes reflect the workplace? Whatever their gender, students are entitled to be equal on their own terms and according to their own needs, and should not be limited by the agenda set by employers. I do not think that colleges actively discriminate by gender, but perhaps inadvertently may support discriminatory practices.

Although colleges may strive for equality in gender issues, this does not imply equality of outcomes and does not presume identical learning experiences for all. What colleges can provide for both male and female students is a fair and just experience for all. For more information, see **Job segregation**.

Giving Feedback – providing information about progress

Whenever you mark or assess anything in college, you provide feedback for your students on their progress. Knowledge of progress is important for sustaining a student's learning, so the more you consider ways of making it meaningful, the better it is for the student.

The first thing is to provide feedback on the actual assignment, project or assessed work. Don't write general things like, 'You did this well', but address the specific point in the assessment that was well done. This means writing something like: 'The essay was well-structured'; 'The design of the project was well-planned and carried out'; 'The presentation was delivered confidently and was well-paced.'

The old advice of writing something positive, then addressing something that needs improving, followed by more positive comments, still holds good today. If you can give examples of ways to improve, then the feedback will be so much the better for the student. The secret is to point out where students can improve – but do it in such a way that they don't give up or get upset. Provide suggestions for improvements that can be incorporated into future assignments. Write feedback clearly and simply, and make sure you keep an electronic copy for your records.

If you are in a position to give verbal feedback to students individually, a good way to start off is by asking the student how they felt they did. You get an idea of how they judge their work and this makes it easier for you to discuss weaknesses. You may have to deal with a student's disappointment and frustration sensitively. It's always much easier to give feedback on the strengths of an assessment.

As an FE lecturer you probably spend a great deal of time giving written feedback to students. Many lecturers store apt phrases and paragraphs and cut and paste them to save time – but remember if feedback is to be of use to students it must be specific to the assignment. There is nothing worse than feedback that doesn't tell students anything about their own work. Knowing how they are getting on and what needs attention helps students focus. If you want your students to improve and achieve, providing meaningful feedback is an excellent way of supporting them. For more information, read the section on **Assessment**.

H is for . . .

HE Supervision – providing guidance and supporting students as they undertake research for a degree.

As the number of students undertaking honours degrees in FE colleges rises, so the number of FE lecturers who are involved in the supervision of a student's research project and assessment of their dissertation increases. The supervisor's role is demanding and requires a fine balance between providing support and guidance and allowing the student to work independently. This balance means you don't undermine the student's autonomy and don't take over the research.

You have to make it explicit to your student what the expectations of the relationship are at the outset, as it differs from the student–lecturer relationship. Establish guidelines so that the student knows how to work with you. This should cover basic things that often cause friction. What is the best time to contact you and where? Can they telephone you at home or only at college? Can they email drafts or do you prefer a printout? Will you be away on holiday at a critical time? Can they contact you as problems arise or must they wait for an appointment? Sort out these questions and prepare a schedule for the first term or semester which is mutually convenient.

Another initial task of the supervisor is to make sure the student is aware of the practical issues entailed for the dissertation to conform to the regulations: the format of the document, number of words required, the positioning of tables and graphs, referencing and what the appendices should contain. At the outset it is also important to clarify other practical issues such as the deadline for submission, the system for second marking, and the number of copies to be printed and bound. Unless these practical issues are spelt out initially, students spend time worrying about them instead of concentrating on the content and academic requirements of the dissertation.

The dissertation is generally an account of a substantial piece of research undertaken by a student as the final part of a degree. Its purpose is to assess the ability of the student to plan and execute an original investigation into a relevant aspect of the subject being studied. The structure of the final report is usually prescribed and will conform to the conventions within the field of study and research methods used. Supervision means ensuring that the student's hypothesis, research question or issue is researchable and manageable, and explaining the intellectual nature of the dissertation for personal or professional development. A supervisor can help negotiate access and give advice about literature searches. Make sure the student prepares a sound proposal at the outset before enthusiastically rushing off and doing a survey or interviewing loads of people. Students are not usually so enthusiastic when they have to re-do something or discard some of their hard work! The research instruments must gather the information the student is seeking and a pilot study checks this.

One of the things most students find difficult to manage is the length of the dissertation and the time it takes to complete. Students have experience of a wide range of assignments, such as essays and projects, but a larger piece of work has, inevitably, to be sub-divided into manageable parts in order to complete it. The component parts of the dissertation must fit well, e.g. research methods must be appropriate to the subject being investigated. The conclusions or recommendations must come out of the data analysis – but, all too often, claims appear at the end of the dissertation and have nothing to do with what has gone on before! All the completed parts need to form a coherent whole and this takes time to bring together. However, it is this final editing and composition that can make the difference between an exceptional dissertation and a middling one. Too often students don't leave time to stand back and appraise the dissertation before the deadline looms. To overcome this, negotiate a schedule with the student and during supervision meetings check how actual progress measures up against it.

An important role for the supervisor is to keep a student motivated. If you are new to HE supervision and worried about whether the work is at the right standard or what mark it warrants, make sure that you talk to someone more experienced. You need support too as you move to HE in FE!

Help – assist a student.

If you ask a student what they want, they say they want 'help'. If they call out in class to attract your attention, students want 'help'. Clearly students think that without your help they cannot get on. Students often feel unable to help themselves. So, when you offer help to students, don't just tell them things, correct mistakes or change things round and sort things out. What would be better is to try and get them to formulate the solutions themselves. This may sound strange when a student obviously can't get on, appears confused or unsure and is just waiting despondently (or impatiently!) for you to go over and help them. What they more than likely want is reassurance and attention. If you can provide this not by 'spoon-feeding' students with information but by encouraging them and motivating them, then your assistance will be all the better – helping students to help themselves!

Humanistic Theories – an approach to education which places the individual at the centre of learning.

Humanistic theories of education place importance on the individual and their personality, i.e. the self, and on the individual in society. Humanistic theories are thus learner-centred and regard group learning highly. It is the active nature of the learning that is stressed, and it is the learner's actions that first and foremost create the learning situation, i.e. it is engaging with the world around them and their position in it that gives rise to the learning environment.

Humanistic theories emphasize the individual's desire for growth and development, and the fulfilment of goals which they set for themselves, whereas Behaviourist theories emphasize the need for stimuli – usually the teacher and the curriculum content. From the humanist viewpoint, learning takes place from drawing on experiences that go to make up 'the self' and the resources of the social context. These experiences and resources comprise life experiences, interpersonal relationships and cultural factors. Thus the motivation for learning comes from the individual, i.e. it is intrinsic. For the FE lecturer, this means accepting students as individuals and respecting their individuality. Rogers' (1983) work generated interest in Humanistic theories in education, and he urges lecturers to be themselves, to be genuine and to treat students with empathy. It is when you begin to drop the façade that you build up as a lecturer, when you stop performing and just be yourself, that you can start to see the value of Humanistic theories as another approach that you could adopt in the education of FE students. See more under **Learning Needs**.

I is for . . .

Icebreakers

You either love them or hate them. Personally, my heart sinks when I'm a member of a group and the group leader introduces a session with an icebreaker. I know that groups have to get started and icebreakers are a way of breaking the initial silence that often hangs over new groups. Getting to know other members of the group is really important and this usually happens over time. If you teach full-time students for the whole academic year then you can all take your time getting to know each other. However, if you teach part-time students or run short training courses of a session or so, then this is not possible.

Choose an icebreaker that everyone can join in – however nervous or confident they are. Using icebreakers that focus on remembering names is advantageous, e.g. getting the group members to write their surname in alphabetical order on the board or flipchart is a simple task. To do this involves group members having to ask each other their surname and mixing together as they get in order. While they're waiting to write their name, they naturally start chatting. If you then ask group members to get in order of their first name and ask the last person in the queue to write the first name against the correct surname, you create a lively atmosphere as they all try to remember, guess or ask each other their surname. This starts a session off well and you have a useful list of names if you need it on the flip chart – handy if you've no register for an initial session!

When students enrol on a new course or join a new group, they arrive at the first session feeling very much like 'newcomers'. They are looking for clues as to how to behave in this new setting, and are thus particularly sensitive to modelling behaviour. This is where the icebreaker such as the one described above comes into its own. If you want students to be active in your sessions, move around, talk to each other, use the flip chart for presentations, etc., then the first session is a really good time to model and encourage such behaviour. Students will absorb what is going on and start to recognize what is considered acceptable behaviour in this group. A desire to become part of the group usually ensures that new members quickly accept how to behave. Joining in allows students to feel part of a group – but be aware that being an outsider is a miserable experience. Make sure students aren't being excluded by language, cultural or social differences.

Icebreakers are meant to make the initial embarrassment of joining a new group a little bit easier. Icebreakers can help students feel good as they get to know each other better. Despite my reserve about icebreakers, I use icebreakers that support learning as new groups start to work together on the task set – especially if icebreakers are fun rather than threatening. Another good one is to ask students to design a medal representing something they were really proud of in the past. When everyone has finished their simple sketch, break the group into threes. One person holds up their medal and the others make comments on it or ask questions about it. This icebreaker gives group members an opportunity to talk about an achievement – be it winning the three-legged race, having twins or rescuing an abandoned kitten! These are all examples used by my students which gave them an opportunity to talk briefly about themselves in a positive fashion and show themselves to others in a good light. If there is time, this can be followed up by getting the group to design a medal which would be presented to them at the end of your course (or event). This encourages students to envisage what they'd like to achieve or become. If they have already revealed something about themselves in the first icebreaker and had an enjoyable time, then students find it easier to share their personal dreams or ambitions. Icebreakers like this one help students get beyond the 'here and now' and begin to think about what it would be possible to achieve in the not too distant future. This is a fun way of beginning action planning or developing learning contracts and makes for a really good start!

Inquiry-based Learning – gaining knowledge through investigating a specific issue.

There are two main ways you can use inquiry-based learning. First, when students are at the beginning of a course, you can devise a case study or scenario which poses a problem or dilemma that needs inquiry to identify how to resolve it. Inquiry-based learning can be devised as a series of vignettes describing people with certain roles or responsibilities and students have to work out how they would deal with a problem – or, better still, role-play them. Inquiry-based learning can be in the form of a description of an ethical issue requiring analysis and resolution. The important thing is that the information must be relevant to the group's vocational or professional area and be up-to-date. You need to provide full details and clear instructions and can use your own knowledge of the workplace – or information gained from current or previous students – to build up the contextual background.

Second, inquiry-based learning is an effective learning tool when students are more confident and experienced, and particularly if they are employed. Such students can develop their own inquiry for a project with a 'real world' problem and then explore it and analyse it for assessment. Using workplace issues as the basis for learning does away with criticisms from employed students that what they do in college is not germane to their organization, and acknowledges the workplace as a source of learning.

As these two examples show, inquiry-based learning is suitable for any level and any stage in a course after students have gained an understanding of the basics of the subject and can recognize the general terminology or language used. Inquiry-based learning can be used in Management and Business Studies courses where strategies to deal with organizational problems can be evaluated and justified. Group projects work well at this level, as 'real world' problems may not be amenable to just one solution and students learn as they exchange ideas and thrash out possible answers. As well as exploring the problem or issue, inquiry-based learning means students may have to resolve conflicts in the group and/or personal clashes – experiences that all help to develop Key Skills.

Students in Foundation Studies can learn through inquiry-based learning as they have to, say, organize a shopping trip to buy the ingredients to make cookies for someone's birthday. Again, it's a 'real world' problem that needs resolving. A group of students on a Childhood Studies course could be provided with a scenario where a toddler in a nursery class shows particular symptoms, e.g. lethargy, grizzling, flushed cheeks. The students can suggest ways of dealing with this when they are responsible for another dozen children in the class. Solutions can be discussed and alternatives imagined without doing any harm to a young child and the importance of getting a proper diagnosis is brought home.

You still have to plan and prepare thoroughly – work out timings, provide sufficient information, make guidelines and instructions clear, identify resources needed – but using inquiry-based learning makes students do the work in sessions, and they enjoy it!

Insight – understanding of a situation.
One of the best things about being a lecturer in an FE college is being in a session when a student suddenly sees the solution to a problem they've been tackling, or out of the blue finds the answer to a question they've struggled to answer. Gestalt psychologists call this 'insight', and witnessing such an incident brings to life the complex process of learning as a student suddenly sees how something they've been grappling with, and which has challenged them, makes sense and they 'get the picture'. It's such a relief for you and the student when 'the penny drops' and they understand something after thinking it through for a time! It's as if everything fits together and now makes more sense and, as a Gestalt psychologist would say, 'the whole is greater than the sum of the parts'.

J is for . . .

Jargon – terminology associated with a specific subject.

Well, as a lecturer, you would call it terminology, wouldn't you! The technical language you use, and with which you are familiar, is often regarded as gobbledygook by students. They start out thinking all these specialist terms are nonsense and question their use. When you give students an information sheet or handout to read on a new topic, or ask them to analyse an article or a chapter, if they can't immediately understand it then they describe it all as waffle! They complain that people should write so that they can understand.

To understand and to extend their knowledge, students need to develop their language skills and recognize more unusual words that they haven't used before and that aren't in everyday use. As a lecturer you can't read a student's mind, so you assess their progress and knowledge by the way they represent it – whether verbally or in writing. The way they use language, and the language they use, reveals their understanding of your subject. So don't apologize for the need to develop language skills, but provide ways to help students to acquire them.

Get students to underline or highlight words they don't know, provide explanations for new words you introduce and put them on the board so that students can see how they are spelt. Share with them that you are still coming across words that you've never heard of before and give examples to encourage them. Get students to start a glossary – that's another word many students aren't familiar with – so they can build up a list of the specialist vocabulary. If you listen, students gradually try out the words they earlier thought of as mumbo-jumbo! They usually spoil the effect by saying they can't pronounce them, but that's OK. When trying out new words, students often say they 'think' it's the right word – and you can reassure them that it is, or if not explain why not and get them to try to substitute a better one. It's encouraging when students start to ask the meanings of words or how to spell them. But the best bit is when you read their assignments or projects and they have competently incorporated so-called jargon into the text!

JISC – the Joint Information Systems Committee.
It's not often that I sing the praises of a committee. But JISC is different. It is a committee set up to provide support for further and higher education by providing – as they say on their website – strategies, guidance, advice and opportunities to use Information and Communication Technology (ICT) to support teaching, learning, research and administration.

The JISC website (www.jisc.ac.uk) provides the latest news in the field and gives advice on how to integrate ICT and e-learning into educational activities. JISC operates through a committee system and is funded by the UK post-16 funding councils to provide regional support for FE colleges, small HE colleges, specialist colleges, sixth-form colleges and Adult and Community Learning providers in England. It's not often that you can say that sounds like money well spent!

Journal Writing – keeping a reflective log.
If you want your students to do well, then a good starting point is to look at what you do as a lecturer. Critical reflection and questioning of practice are a basis for professional development for lecturers. Journal writing involves reflecting on your teaching and learning and can lead to systematically questioning your teaching strategies and methods and your students' learning. One way of evaluating what you do is through completion – and later examination – of a journal (Bolton, 2001; Moon, 1999).

The act of writing is important. You may select a special notebook for the journal and jot down your thoughts as they occur or when you have time to sit and reflect. Journal writing may just be done occasionally when a particular event makes you stop and think about an aspect of teaching and learning. Alternatively, the journal may be in the form of a diary which you write regularly. If you choose an A4 diary with a day-to-a-page this means you can enter tutorial appointments, meetings and timetabled sessions and still have room to write up evaluations of the tutorials and meetings and make notes about how the sessions went. This is a good way of keeping all your records and reflective writing in one place.

The journal doesn't have to be in the form of a book. You could set up an online journal if this suits you better, and keep it in a separate folder on your computer or link it with your timetables and course records and keep your journal entries with them. The way you undertake your journal writing is not the critical thing. The critical thing is that you do it!

If you choose a way of journal writing that suits you then you've a better chance of continuing the practice and fitting it into your busy day. If you set aside time to do this daily, you can capture how you felt after, say, a particularly bad session. You can record ideas for amending session plans and ways of doing things differently while things are still fresh in your mind. When writing about critical incidents that caused you anxiety or were stressful, record what happened before the incident, describe the incident as fully as you can, and then record what happened afterwards. Writing a journal in this way helps you to become aware of what triggers critical incidents for you, e.g. it may be when you feel threatened by students' questions, can't handle disagreements between students or try to fit too much into a session and panic. This highlights something practical to work on for your professional development.

If you experience problems with a particular student, it might be a good idea to include a profile of incidents relating specifically to that student in your journal writing. In this way you can over, say, a term, build up a picture of the problems you confront with that student. Be careful not to include names in case you leave your journal around or someone can get access to your computer area. Journal writing is a way of giving attention to your thoughts and feelings. However, journal writing is not like writing to an 'agony aunt' for advice: you write the journal to generate your own 'advice'. For example, after each session with a student you have problems with, record your reflections in your journal. Your critical evaluation of the entries at the end of the term may illuminate why things went wrong, e.g. what frustrates them, what frustrates you, etc. You use your own 'advice' to plan next term's sessions.

When lecturers undertake journal writing as part of a teacher education or professional development programme there is a tendency to dwell on things that went wrong rather than write about things that really worked and were successful. If you find that you are getting too introspective, or can't seem to find solutions through examining your journal writing after a period of time, then talk to a colleague and share your concerns. Two heads are often better than one in such situations!

Another practical way of using your journal writing is when you are preparing final evaluations for your course. A quick flick through the journal soon reminds you of a problem with rooming or resources, or makes you aware just how much a student has done to overcome problems that only a little while ago seemed insurmountable.

If you persist with your journal writing, you may find that your systematic questioning changes. Instead of questioning what you have done wrong, you may start to frame questions such as what is wrong with the system.

If you offer journal writing as part of a programme for your students, do make it clear to them if it is to be submitted as part of an assignment, i.e. is it to be a dialogue journal that passes from the writer to a lecturer. It makes a big difference to the journal writer if they know someone will read their entries. Journal extracts can be used for evaluation and analysis without the whole journal being submitted and just using extracts or quoting passages. So make it clear to students what is to happen before they start journal writing.

K is for . . .

Key Skills

Key skills are an attempt to bridge the gap between what students learn in college and what is actually required of them to be successful in the workplace. Employers increasingly felt that when students left college, their skills were inadequate and ineffective for the modern workplace, in which hi-tech and service industries were progressively replacing the traditional manufacturing industries that had once been the backbone of the UK economy. Changes in the nature of employment in the UK during the last 20 years or so mean that the vocational and personal skills required by the workforce are also changing. The instigation of key skills was driven by employers and supported by trade unions. Initially, a range of common skills needed for employment in these emerging sectors of industry was identified. These were subsequently labelled 'core skills', and re-named 'key skills'. Dearing's Review of Qualifications for 16–19 Year Olds (1996) recommended that key skills should be available across academic and work-based education and training. Key skills qualifications at levels 1–4 are communication, application of number, and information and communication technology. The units are achieved by portfolio and testing. Also available are wider key skills units: working with others, improving own learning and performance and problem solving. These are achieved by assessment of a portfolio. Additionally, there is a key skills unit at level 5 in personal skills development.

Current key skills standards and guidance for tutors and assessors is available on the QCA website: www.qca.org.uk.

Knowledge – theoretical or practical understanding

The nature of knowledge is important to consider if you want to understand how students learn and construct their own knowledge, and also how you as an FE lecturer learn and develop your professional knowledge. However, the variety of descriptions of knowledge, and the terms used to discuss it often mean that lecturers switch off when authors theorize about knowledge. Take 'epistemology', for example. All this really means is the theory of knowledge. The question is, how do we know how things really are or how things really work? How do we know what constitutes warrantable or legitimate knowledge? What about 'ontology'? Again, it is concerned with abstract things and the essence of things. So, is knowledge a given out there in the world or is it created by one's own mind? Obviously these are complex questions and warrant more than a simple explanation – but that will suffice for now as I don't want you to switch off!

Knowledge can be explicit, i.e. you know that you know something! It is clear to you and others that you plainly recognize or understand something. Or knowledge can be tacit and you are unaware that you know something, or find it difficult to explain to others what you know. Look out for examples of this when discussing projects or assignments with students in tutorials. You may ask them what they know about a particular idea introduced in your course and be met with a blank look. However, when you prompt students or suggest examples that might be relevant, more often than not they say 'you mean so-and-so ...' and can draw on examples from their previous experience, study or workplace practice. Purposive questioning is a tool lecturers can use to help students make tacit knowledge explicit and thus enable them to connect their previous experiences and knowledge with their current college work.

Knowledge can be propositional, or public, and this means that others have developed ideas or theories and written about them and published them. These authors have put their knowledge in the public domain where it can be accessed by others, either through textbooks, professional and academic journals, websites or conferences. Theoretical knowledge about teaching and learning made public in this way is often regarded by lecturers as removed from the everyday reality of their practice of teaching and supporting students' learning. Yet, acquisition of theoretical knowledge is gained not just through accessing others' theories but also through the way we interpret and experience our practice. By that I mean, the way lecturers go about teaching and learning and the choices made in day-to-day work are based on some idea, belief, or value, i.e. some personal theory.

Practical knowledge is gained from reflecting on your own experiences and thinking about how you can, for example, teach more effectively in the future. The knowledge you gain from your reflections has also been termed 'expressive knowledge', as you are able to construct and express it after your deliberations (Willis, 1999). This is a particularly good definition as it conveys not just that you can articulate the knowledge derived from purposeful reflection on your experiences or problems, but also that what you have gained from the activity is meaningful and significant to you and your practice.

The nature of knowledge gets more complicated when authors start talking about how we get to know about knowledge. 'Metacognition' is literally knowledge of knowledge. It is associated with learning to learn and concerns the awareness and control we have over our own thinking. This idea is demonstrated very well by the concept of 'control knowledge', which is a holistic way of defining how we develop self-knowledge through self-awareness, self-management and self-evaluation, etc. It is the knowledge gained from all the separate bits of self-knowledge that contribute to an overarching knowledge, which Eraut (1994) defines as control knowledge.

The use of different terminology for the nature of knowledge is not new. The Ancient Greeks identified a form of knowledge as 'techne', which we talk about as the technical knowledge involved in knowing how to do something. In everyday terms we call this 'know-how', e.g. planning a session and delivering it, which involves knowing the theory of what constitutes a good session and being able to carry it out in practice. What works, and what makes good teaching in FE, is influenced by knowing many factors – level of group, number and disposition of students, teaching methods, subject content – but it is not a set formula that can be simply applied like a set of instructions or a recipe.

I could go on! What you may find after reading this is that you now become aware of different sorts of knowledge and suddenly you'll find them jumping off the page at you: instrumental knowledge, communicative knowledge, emancipatory knowledge. I bet you can add more to the list!

Kolb's Learning Cycle

For FE lecturers, Kolb's Learning Cycle is surely one of the most familiar theoretical models of learning (Kolb, 1984). The model is based on a notion of four stages within experiential learning: a concrete or actual experience; reflective observation on that experience; analysis of and theorizing about the experience; and using the conclusion to test out in new situations. The four-stage cycle is then repeated and the stages completed again. It is possible to start at any of the four stages of the cycle but, according to the theory, a whole cycle must be completed for learning to be effective.

For many educationists this is too simple a model of learning, and even Kolb accepted that people do not pay equal attention to each stage of the cycle. From this, Kolb concluded that people mainly used whichever one of the four stages suited their ability and disposition, i.e. their learning style (for more information on this read, about learning styles such as **Visual, Auditory, Kinaesthetic** V). If this is the case, to all intents and purposes, the cycle is not as predictive of effective learning as it suggests. To overcome this, an FE lecturer needs to get across to students that just engaging in an activity, e.g. reading a chapter, completing a diagram, photographing an image or planning a menu, will not necessarily in itself be an effective learning experience. What makes it effective for students is thinking about how they did something and why. This reflection and observation can be prompted by the student or by a lecturer's response, feedback or questioning.

Students are encouraged to draw conclusions from the experience, e.g. the image was not in focus or the menu contained two fish dishes. If the conclusion arrived at is made explicit, then the student is able independently to make use of this learning when taking another photograph or planning a new menu. In this way, lecturers can encourage students to use all the four stages of the cycle and develop a range of approaches to learning, e.g. think about what happened before rushing on to the next activity and experiencing the same problems again.

L is for . . .

Learning Needs – what students require to make progress
As an FE lecturer you are always being urged to take students' learning needs into account. You are exhorted to identify your students' learning needs, particularly their motivation for enrolling on your course, so that you can support their learning effectively. Lecturers are always being told by students what they 'want' – but how do we know what students' 'needs' are?

I would question whether it is possible to take into account every student's individual learning needs in an average group. Not all students have a clear idea of their motivations, and this may be because these are intangible and difficult to identify or hard to express, e.g. personal growth or change. Even when students do identify their learning needs, they may have such diverse and dissimilar goals and aspirations that you would be hard-pushed to meet all their individual learning needs in one of your sessions. This does not mean that you should not discuss them or acknowledge them and use a variety of methods in sessions to accommodate different learning needs. What it does mean is that you have to know how to create the conditions needed for learning if you want active participation and commitment from students.

Maslow (1954) identified a hierarchy of five levels of innate needs, which he associated with motivation. He argued that people have inherent wants; they always want more, and what they want depends on what they already have. Still with me?

People can be pretty sceptical about this hierarchy and the claim that we have a fundamental need to develop our capabilities to their full potential. This notion is described as self-actualization, and at No. 1 is at the top of the Maslow's hierarchy of innate needs. Even Maslow admits not everyone reaches this peak, so let's start our countdown from the bottom of the hierarchy!

At No. 5 are physiological needs, i.e. for water, food, air, sleep and sexual expression. These are closely followed at No. 4 by safety needs, i.e. shelter, order, security, comfort, freedom from fear and threat. If needs at these first two levels aren't satisfied, our life is in danger. Even though their condition is far from life-threatening, if your students are hungry, thirsty, cold or tired, you cannot get them to concentrate on their college work. All the students can think of is having a break to buy a snack and drink – or start eating and drinking in class, which many colleges frown on. One thing you can be sure of is that at that moment they are probably not contemplating how to develop their capabilities to their full potential, and are not at all motivated by your remonstrations not to give up and finish their task before they have a break.

At No. 3 are affiliation needs, i.e. belonging, affection, love and relationships. This level of needs is also important for lecturers to be aware of, because if these needs are not met, students feel inferior and helpless, whereas if they are met, confidence develops. Again, esteem needs at No. 2 have resonance for your students. They include the need for recognition, attention and appreciation. I bet you have dealt with students who always want to be noticed and need constant attention in sessions. Perhaps you feel like 'quashing' them to let others have a look-in. Interestingly, Maslow points out that self-esteem must not be based solely on respect for self but also respect for others, and this knowledge has helped me understand how to deal with attention-seekers.

Well, we're back at No. 1 again. The hierarchy is supposed to represent a life-time development, so it's not surprising that you don't find everyone motivated to achieve their full potential in your sessions. If you accept that these needs are not uniform and that people tend to shuttle between the levels, then it may help you create the conditions for learning. Why not test it out? If your students are becoming restless, send them for a coffee break and they should come back highly motivated. Well, I did say there is scepticism about the theory!

Learning Styles – favouring different ways of learning.
Individuals are said to have a preferred learning style. However, there is a lot of controversy about learning styles. It is interesting that one of the meanings of 'style' is 'fashion' and it seems to me that, at one moment, learning styles are all the fashion and everyone eagerly assesses them and then, the next moment, it seems that researchers aren't so sure that particular preferences link to a student's subject choice or the way they choose to study.

Honey and Mumford's (1986) questionnaire has proved highly popular and identifies the characteristics of preferred learning styles for each respondent. These are linked to Kolb's (1986) cycle of experiential learning (see **Kolb's Learning Cycle**). Basically, if you complete Honey and Mumford's questionnaire you can discover if your are a 'diverger' who learns best by reflecting on experiences, an 'assimilator' who learns best by thinking and theorizing, a 'converger' who learns best by problem-solving or an 'accommodator' who learns more intuitively.

You are probably aware that different students approach your sessions in different ways. The important thing is to get to know your students and make sure your teaching encourages learning – so look under **Teaching Style** to find out more.

LSN – the Learning and Skills Network.
In April 2006 the Learning and Skills Development Agency (LSDA) evolved into two organizations. One is the Quality Improvement Agency for Lifelong Learning (QIA), and the other is the Learning and Skills Network (LSN). The Network is responsible for research, training and consultancy work

within Learning and Skills sector. If you want to keep up to date with the 'hot' issues in FE, then visit the LSN website. You can access loads of free newsletters, pamphlets and reports about current projects and policies in the sector at www.lsn.org.uk.

Level Indicators – ranking of qualifications.
The level indicators in the revised National Qualifications Framework provide a guide for students, lecturers, employers and parents to the range of qualifications and levels available. Level indicators describe the learning and achievement that happens at each level and show how the skills and knowledge relate to job roles. There are nine levels, from Entry to Level 8. From 2006, students completing higher level qualifications will receive certificates at the revised levels 4–8.

Although the structure has been revised, the level indicators reveal the inconsistency in titles. Qualification titles such as 'certificate' and 'diploma' are not indicators of level but a choice of the awarding body. For example, you could achieve a Diploma for Beauty Specialists at Level 2 (equivalent to GCSEs A*–C), or a Diploma in Translation at Level 7 (equivalent to Masters degrees). Current information can be found on the QCA's website: www.qca.org.uk.

Low Achievers – students who have little success in making progress.
When a student is struggling, the temptation is to take control and tell them what to do rather than help them to learn skills to take responsibility for their own learning. When a student feels a failure, normal dialogue is often not possible. Students are often surly and clam up when they get poor results, and they don't attend tutorials you've arranged to try and help them. You have to make contact somehow – even if it means catching them in the corridor, or phoning them. The important thing when a student is disillusioned and it's difficult to have a reasonable and rational conversation is to try to open up an understanding of each other's feelings: your

concerns and their disappointments. Students who are not achieving often feel that they have not only let themselves down, but also let others down. You can't force students to attend more or make more effort, but sometimes just the fact that they can turn to someone for support makes the difference between them giving up and giving it a go.

M is for ...

Mentor – adviser, counsellor, guide, tutor, teacher.
Mentoring schemes have been set up in many colleges, for peer support of both staff and students. However, the mentoring role can be interpreted widely (as the definition above shows), and what a mentor does varies from college to college and even from person to person. This is not a criticism, but rather a strength of mentoring.

Mentors help facilitate change in others, who are very often their peers, and so the mentoring relationship is crucial if change is going to happen. Research that is very applicable here took place in a college of Further and Higher Education within a mentoring scheme set up to help the induction of new teaching staff, and revealed that there was a continuum of mentoring styles (Woodd, 2001). The role could be that of a 'buddy', i.e. a befriending and information-giving role. A lecturer in that role would act as an induction mentor who showed new colleagues how things were done. This description would fit the role of 'buddy' played by students, too.

The next point on the continuum is an 'organizer', who acts as a subject mentor, i.e. as a critical friend, coaching, providing examples from experiences and giving feedback. Again, you could easily apply this to student buddies who act as coaches. The 'facilitator' acts as a career mentor, which requires a deeper relationship built on trust and empathy. Perhaps this is the point where student buddies should be advised to refer students on to appropriate professionals.

The research clearly shows the mentor can be dynamic and change styles according to the needs of the situation and urgency of the problem. Woodd's framework setting out full information about mentoring styles (Woodd, 2001) would make worthwhile reading if you are a mentor or are considering taking on the role.

Methods – ways of teaching and learning.

The methods you use in teaching and learning send messages to students about the types of learners you expect them to be. The trouble is that there is a tendency to choose what suits you as a lecturer rather than what suits the students. You bring your ideas, theories and personality to the classroom and the students bring with them their own ideas and dispositions. These facets of the teaching and learning environment are dynamic, which is why it is impossible to say one method is right and another method is wrong. What you can say is that students depend on you to create a learning environment that supports their learning, and this means that you have to make some decisions – even if the decision is to let students take more and more of the decisions!

This suggests that the main factors are about structure and control: how much and who takes it. Elliott (1991) provides a practical theory to help you when considering structure. He identifies three main dimensions of teaching and learning. The first dimension is 'formal informal', i.e. the degree of dependence or independence of students on the lecturer's position of authority. The second dimension is 'structured unstructured', i.e. whether the teaching and learning environment is subject-centred and concerned with outcomes or student-centred and concerned with process. The third dimension is 'directed-guided open ended', i.e. whether the lecturer's methods are prescribed in advance, responsive to problems perceived by students or whether the lecturer refrains from imposing constraints on students' abilities to direct their own learning. You may use methods which lie across the three dimensions and may vary where you are in a dimension from time to time, according to your topic and your student group.

You have to acknowledge how you structure your sessions and your position in these three main dimensions before you select your methods. Your choice of methods links to who takes control, and Minton (2005) provides an excellent framework to choose from, which is popular with FE lecturers as your decisions are easier to make. He lists the methods on a continuum: 'teacher control–least control'. The continuum starts with most teacher control, e.g. lecture, demonstration, structured discussion. It then moves to unstructured discussion, seminar, tutorial – which means less control. Next is shared control in practicals, simulation and games, role-play, resource-based learning, films/TV and visits. Student control comes into play at the other end of the continuum with distance learning/flexi-study, discovery project/research and real-life experience.

Can you now see that the methods you use in teaching and learning send messages to students about the types of learners you expect them to be? These two practical theories should help you to choose what to use in an informed way.

Multiple Intelligences

The theory of multiple intelligences was published by Howard Gardner over a two decades ago (Gardner, 1983). His evidence from people in different walks of life, including groups of bright children and adults with special learning needs, was that a strength (or weakness) in one area did not necessarily mean a strength (or weakness) in another area. From further research, he developed the notion that intelligence was not one intellectual capacity and at that time identified seven separate intelligences: verbal-linguistic; mathematical-logical; musical; visual-spatial; bodily-kinaesthetic; interpersonal; and intra-personal-reflective. Later he identified two more intelligences: naturalistic and existential (Gardner, 1999).

Each intelligence, Gardner asserted, was genetically pre-programmed and so an individual's capacity is reflected by the extent each one of the intelligences is exhibited, e.g. if your strength was musical intelligence then you would excel at playing an instrument or singing. In general terms, you might say you had a gift for music. This idea, although contentious when introduced, has had a considerable impact on the education of school children but as yet has not really influenced teaching and learning in FE colleges to the same extent. Yet the concept that individual differences affect what we are good at and what we gravitate towards is an important one to consider in vocational education and training. Are students drawn to a particular vocational area because of their innate intelligence in a particular area – or are other educational, social and economic factors responsible?

The idea that the ability to learn is dependent on a single, fixed and quantifiable capacity is now generally rejected. It is apparent to any FE lecturer that students differ and learn differently, and the theory of multiple intelligences offers a useful framework to support those who find conventional and traditional teaching strategies and classroom settings difficult to get on with. Educational success relies heavily on linguistic and mathematical/logical intelligences. This means that students whose strengths lie in other intelligences often struggle or feel excluded from classes where the focus is on the written word, e.g. reading and note-taking, or demands reasoning skills involving number, e.g. analysing, comparing evaluating. The lecturer can help students in two ways. First, help them develop intelligences that are weaker, e.g. give them specific things to look for in a passage set for reading; provide handouts for note-taking which just have headings so that students have direction about what is important to record. Rather than use a textbook all the time, use written material that is derived from the workplace, specialist magazines or newspapers and encourage students to start a word list with meanings of significant words.

Second, help students by the wider use of graphical and artistic representations. Resources such as pictures, photographs, charts and posters help stimulate learning. You could use more drama and role-play, less talk and chalk and more discussion. Help students by encouraging them to write 'stories' when problem-solving, e.g. what if ...? This encourages them to use their imagination and requires reflection. These methods of teaching and learning encourage active participation and offer students with different strengths and weaknesses an opportunity to discover that they can be successful and demonstrate their learning in less conventional ways.

The key idea that is worth taking from the theory of multiple intelligences is the argument for abandoning fixed ideas of ability in favour of recognizing more than one view of intelligence, which calls for a variety of teaching methods.

N is for . . .

National Qualifications Framework

The National Qualifications Framework is a grid of accredited qualifications which sets out the levels at which qualifications can be recognized in England, Wales and Northern Ireland. The idea behind the framework is that it helps students make informed decisions about qualifications they need. Students can compare the levels of different qualifications and identify progression routes to the career they are considering. When comparing qualifications, students need to bear in mind that they are comparable only in general level of outcome, not that they have the same outcome.

The NQF has undergone revision and the key change from 2006 is that the number of levels in the framework has increased to nine: entry Level to Level 8. Entry Level to Level 3 stays the same. However, to permit comparison with the framework for higher education qualifications (FHEQ), the original Levels 4 and 5 have been revised to Levels 4–8. Level 4 is equivalent to HE C (certificate); Level 5 is equivalent to HE I (Intermediate); Level 6 is equivalent to HE H (honours); Level 7 is equivalent to HE M (masters) and Level 8 is equivalent to HE D (doctoral). For current information access the QCA's website: www.qca.org.uk.

New Technology – innovative equipment which can be used as a learning resource.

Say what you like, but new technology has already had an impact on teaching and learning in colleges. Has adopting new technology improved your teaching and learning? What is new technology exactly and what do you call it? Is it Information and Learning Technology (ILT), Information and Communication Technology (ICT), e-learning, blended learning, Virtual Learning Environments (VLE), Managed Learning Environments (MLE), and/or Augumented Learning Environments?

Whether you are familiar with new technology or not, or whatever you call it, you have to accept that life is changing. The reality is that virtually all FE students are familiar with new technology, particularly younger students and those working in environments using information technology. They have access to – or may own – a personal computer which they use for college work and for sending emails as well as for chat lines and games. They probably have access to the internet and possibly broadband and use a mobile phone not just for chatting but for texting, taking photos and getting information. Younger students are probably more familiar with the basic tools for e-learning than lecturers and many students have a sophisticated understanding of new technology through their workplace – and that could be a problem. You can't sit back forever and ignore the enormous changes in technology that are increasingly affecting teaching and learning.

Your college classrooms may be digital already, with smartboards, digital cameras and access to an intranet. You may still need advice about how to use these expertly, and many colleges now have an ILT/e-learning champion who will be able to help you, recommend learning packages and provide assistance with developing your ideas or instruction about facilities available within your college.

New technology has the potential to change the way lecturers and students work, which means most lecturers have to become learners again. Although most lecturers have probably attended some form of ILT updating and development, ILT use has usually been associated with saving money on teaching and learning rather than investing in teaching and learning. New technology is not the answer to the economic problems of a cash-strapped college, which allows them to do away with the need for lecturers and classroom space. E-learning needs to be looked on as an approach which supports teaching and learning and is integrated into wider curriculum development. E-learning requires a new mindset. Of course, you will have to develop your own technological skills. However, the biggest thing you will have to do is grasp the fact that the roles of lecturers and students will change. A good way of starting with new technology is to develop your methods of curriculum delivery rather than try to find commercially produced instructional programmes.

New technology enables you to help students both with their educational achievement and organizational skills. Educationally, e-learning fits well with current ideas about learning and teaching in FE, e.g. notions of encouraging student autonomy. You will not be the sole source of knowledge but someone who supports a student's learning. New technology gives you flexibility, e.g. you can work with a small group face-to-face while the rest of the group work individually on self-directed resources that you have developed.

Developing resources does not always have to be time-consuming if you have a heavy workload. Use the case studies that you already have, rework handouts by just adding questions, set research tasks on specific topics, use all the activities/exercises previously used in class and provide instruction so that the students can complete them independently.

Organizationally, if you put course material on an intranet you can forget about the need to photocopy handouts. If students are away, they can still get the information they missed. Details of assignments and assessment procedures can be available for students. They can access assessment and examination criteria and become familiar with them. Students can email their work and you can email their feedback to them. You can use bulletin boards to contact students easily, e.g. if there is a room change or a tutorial is required.

If you are anxious about new technology, just remember that there are loads of simple ways (like the examples above) in which you can gradually incorporate new technology into your curriculum. Don't be afraid to swap roles with your students and learn from them. If you are an ICT lecturer, you will already know how exciting new technology can be – but remember other colleagues might appreciate your help, not just your students!

In the early part of your programme, you have to ensure that students have the requisite skills in place. You can make the most of peer-coaching and sharing of information in initial induction sessions and provide step-by-step prompt-sheets for those who need them. Once students are confident, the important thing is to use the new technology as much as you can and ditch outdated practices. For more information, see Whalley *e-learning in FE*.

Noise Levels

You spend half of your time trying to get students to talk, and the other half of the time getting them to keep quiet. When students get together at the beginning of your session and start swapping stories about what they did last night, chatting about arrangements for lunchtime or planning tonight's activities, the noise level rises. If you shout over the noise to make them keep quiet you only increase the level.

Over the years, I have found that the noise level generally subsides pretty quickly and I would advise any new lecturer not to panic about noise at the beginning of the session. After all, you probably chat to others when you first meet them – it's just when a large group does this it gets noisy. If you make it clear that you are ready to start by being assertive and standing in front of the class, they will soon get the message that you mean business and want the session to begin. It's only when you come into the room, start fiddling around with notes and handouts and fixing the blinds or finding resources that students don't get the signal that you're ready to start. If the class is boisterous, take the register formally to calm things down. Then start your session straight away, before they've got time to continue their conversations. It may take a bit of time, but gradually a practical routine can be established even for a rowdy group.

What is acceptable as a tolerable noise level in a session varies from lecturer to lecturer. However, there appears to be a 'magic' level which a 'good' lecturer should not allow the group to exceed. I don't know who came up with this unspoken standard but I've noticed it in lots of colleges. As soon as the noise can be described as a 'din' or 'racket', other lecturers feel duty bound to talk about it in the staffroom or confront the students in another session. What they rarely do is intervene and offer to help.

Noise levels do affect the learning environment, so you do need to address them. Don't remonstrate with the whole group, but speak to students individually if their noise is disturbing others. Expect students to respect you and others in the group and don't treat loud-mouthed comments as a joke. You don't need students to work in silence – but you do need them to work. There is nothing more rewarding than listening to the low buzz of noise you get in a group when they are all happily working away. For more on this, see **Behaviour**.

O is for . . .

Ofsted – Office for Standards in Education.

Ofsted is now responsible for inspecting sixth-form, tertiary, general further education and specialist colleges. The Adult Learning Inspectorate currently undertakes joint inspections with Ofsted of colleges where there are significant numbers of learners over 19 years of age. The current inspection cycle for FE colleges is 2005–09, and a key feature of this cycle is annual assessment visits made to all colleges. These visits review college performance using students' achievements and other data, and help Ofsted determine the basis and time of the next inspection. High performing colleges may not be subject to a full inspection whereas inadequate colleges will be inspected more frequently and by a larger inspection team.

New measures of success are being developed by the LSC in conjunction with Ofsted to provide more comprehensive indicators of achievement, linking outcomes to the previous attainment of learners. Perhaps this development will lessen the fear and dread surrounding inspection which is currently palpable in the FE sector. As part of the Education and Inspections Bill (DfES, 2006), several existing inspectorates will merge. Inspection services for children, young people and adult learners are being reformed through the creation of a single organization to be called the Office for Standards in Education, Children's Services and Skills. The Adult Learning Inspectorate is brought within the remit of Ofsted and the QIA has the role of commissioning quality improvement work in the Learning and Skills sector. More information about Ofsted and information about colleges can be found on www.ofsted.gov.uk/colleges.

OLASS – Offender Learning and Skills Service.

Prison education is an often forgotten part of post-compulsory education, and has suffered upheaval in recent years. In December 2005, the government published a Green Paper, 'Reducing Re-Offending through Skills and Employment'. The Green Paper set out a joint strategy produced by the DfES, the Home Office and the Department for Work and Pensions (DfES, 2005). Despite the uncertainties in the sector over contracts and the fact that the majority of lecturers in prison education are part-time or sessional, the Green Paper proposes a radical vision for change in which the emphasis will be on improving skills and employment opportunities for offenders.

The proposals are exemplary, e.g. a focus on employment; integration of learning and skills into sentence planning which includes a learning contract; establishing an offender learner 'campus'; more focus on 16 and 17 year olds. Evidence suggests that employment and a reduction in re-offending are linked and that stability and quality of employment are key factors. However, it is recognized that the challenge is a stark one. Whether lecturers will have the energy and enthusiasm to realize this vision, and whether funding materializes, are two questions that still need addressing. Let's hope the consultative stage of the Green Paper raises these questions.

One-to-one Tutorials – working with students individually.

All lecturers will probably be involved in one-to-one tutorials at some point in the academic year. One-to-one tutorials are a feature of provision in the FE sector and are a constituent part of a learner-centred approach to education. The role of tutor is central to successful learning.

You need to prepare for tutorials just as you do for your sessions – and you have to get students to prepare as well. Both tutor and student should have a shared understanding of the purpose of the proposed tutorial and negotiate and set an agenda, or SMART targets.

Tutorials can be used for a variety of purposes: personal, academic or disciplinary. They can be student-led or tutor-led. You might ask 'at risk' students to attend or students might ask for a tutorial when they need extra help. The important thing for the tutor to remember is that even if you requested a student to come for a tutorial, you are still responding to the student's issues. Although you need some of the skills of a counsellor, e.g., listening skills, summarizing and reflecting back, you are not a counsellor. Emotional issues affect learning and inevitably these have to be addressed. You need to acknowledge a student's feelings and help them confront challenges or conflicts that impact on their college work. Students respond to positive feedback and praise, and you want students to end the tutorial feeling confident of their ability to succeed. However, if emotional issues are preventing dialogue about a student's work, then it is more appropriate to refer them to the college counsellor.

One-to-one tutorials are an opportunity for getting to know students and an opportunity for students to talk and tutors to listen. As students identify areas of success and areas of development, they engage in self-assessment and develop skills that are useful academically and in the workplace.

Tutors must keep a record of tutorials: summarize, identify action points and track progress. Tutorial systems in a college can nurture or constrain a student's learning processes. Make sure you don't waste tutorial time and use one-to-one tutorials to good effect. A publication by LSDA (Green, 2002) has lots of practical advice on this.

P is for . . .

Paperwork

Does paperwork get you down? I'd be surprised if it didn't, as the amount of paperwork required in the FE sector nowadays is massive. Lecturers complain that paperwork takes their time away from tasks they consider more important – like preparation and marking. If you are getting bogged down by documents that need completing, consider the following. Foucault thought that our documentation is part of our professional practice (Fillingham, 1993). He thought paperwork was not to be despised. Yet, we all probably loathe and detest it. Many see paperwork as something for others to measure us by. Managers, inspectors and government officials demand audits, evaluations, planning profiles, targets, reports and registers. As a philosopher, Foucault regarded paperwork as an intrinsic part of what we do and necessary evidence of what we do. *Your* paperwork provides evidence of quality in education. It is a constitutive part of who you are and what you do. Does that make you look at the pile of forms on your desk waiting to be completed, and the documents waiting to be read, in a different way? Does that help you look at paperwork more sympathetically because it represents the quality of your teaching? Perhaps, not! I suspect Foucault did not have to complete as many forms or read as many reports as an FE lecturer does!

Passport to Teaching Award – a step to full Qualified Teacher Learning and Skills (QTLS).

As part of a new qualification process for teachers in the

Learning and Skills sector, all teachers will be given an initial assessment leading to an individual learning plan. The next step in the qualification, effective in 2007, is the Passport to Teaching Award. This is a programme of approximately 30 guided learning hours plus teaching practice and observation, which everyone teaching in the sector will have to achieve. Subject-specific and generic mentors provide support for teachers undertaking the Passport to Teaching Award. There is an emphasis on practical expertise, which will be assessed by observation, appraisal and mentor reports at Level 3. Only those with a limited teaching role may exit the qualification process at this stage. To find out more about the full qualification, look under **Teaching Qualifications**.

Planning Programmes – preparing a series of sessions in a course.

Before you can go very far in planning programmes, you have to think about your overall aims for the course. These are probably long-term goals, i.e. they embrace the reasons you are teaching in FE, which are generally not made explicit. Clarifying these overall aims enables you to choose appropriate teaching–learning strategies. One example would be that if you have an overall aim of encouraging student autonomy, then teaching–learning strategies must not encourage dependency on you.

A variety of approaches to teaching–learning – e.g. presentations, seminars, demonstrations, quizzes, visits and tutorials – should be adopted during the course to achieve a balance between content delivery and student engagement. What is required of students during the programme is as much a part of the teaching–learning experience as the subject content. This includes the standards by which students' work is assessed and also the methods of assessment, which must be congruent with the aims. It is important to bear in mind your long-term goals while trying to help students achieve short-term goals within a session or series of sessions, e.g. to develop a particular skill or understand a specific concept.

Planning programmes is one of the most demanding tasks a lecturer has to undertake. This is because so many different aspects of teaching and learning have to be taken into account. The challenge is to make all these aspects link together and fall into place in the programme. It's not just methods you have to think about, but resources, assessment design, group size and capability. This requires solving a lot of problems. You have to take decisions about where to pitch the level, what pace would suit, how to sequence sessions and about coverage of the content. You have to decide on the overall design. Do you start from what they know and then address the unknown? Do you begin with concrete concepts and move to abstract ones? Do you use a chronological order or do you use themes? Or, do you start with what you feel confident to deliver?

A model that fits well with most programmes and has stood the test of time is planning a spiral curriculum (Bruner, 1977). This means that learning has to be constantly revisited and supports the acquisition of skills and knowledge as a process of growth and development. When planning programmes, you have to take into account that achieving the course aims will not be straightforward, as students learn by fits and starts and so developing and re-developing learning is important. Planning programmes is demanding, but that makes the task a really good way of developing your professional skills and knowledge. You have to deliberate about what you value in teaching and learning and think hard about how you can achieve this.

PCE – Post-compulsory Education.
The FE sector is frequently described as post-compulsory education. This implies that the sector's provision is exclusively for those over the school-leaving age of 16. However, more and more those still attending school also attend college for part of the school week. School pupils aged 14 to 16 can elect to take vocational qualifications and opt out of part of the National Curriculum. Perhaps we should drop the term 'PCE' in future. For more information, look under **Young Learners**.

Q is for . . .

QCA – Qualifications and Curriculum Authority.
The QCA is a public body whose board members are appointed by the Secretary of State for Education and Skills. It monitors qualifications in colleges and in the workplace and has responsibility for reforming the 14 to 19 curriculum so that it is flexible and overcomes the traditional academic/vocational divide.

Quality Evaluation – ascertaining the excellence of students' experience at college.
How many times have you spent time going through students' evaluation forms, worrying over them, summarizing them and developing an action plan – and then nothing happens! Once they're fed into the college system, they seem to fall into a black hole. You can't automatically expect extra tutorial time because that was in your action plan, or hope to be timetabled in a better room – even if these things will improve the quality of your course. If you want your students' experiences of your course to be good, or you want things improved, you have to be realistic and do something about it yourself. I could suggest that you hassle your managers and start a campaign for items to be put in the budget, and bring up the issues at every meeting. Structures and resources do contribute to quality and you have to be aware of the way the system works, but I suggest to you it would be wiser and less of a hassle to expend your efforts where they are important for you – in the classroom with your students.
   There is a tendency to think of quality evaluation taking

place at the end of a course or event. But this does not have to be the case. Evaluation does not only have to be a formal affair that feeds into the college's quality assurance process. The best evaluation is informal and ongoing. If you want to know what your students think about their course, then just talk to them about it or ask their opinion on aspects of the course. When you introduce a new task or project, check your students' reactions straight away. Where students appear disinterested in a part of the curriculum, seek their views on what might work better. When students are critical or start complaining about things, try to get them to be specific and come up with some ideas for improvement themselves. Spend time talking to students about things that are important to you and to them, i.e. your teaching and their learning.

Even if you involve students more and try to meet their needs, you must recognize that you can't please everyone all the time. Like me, perhaps you have changed things in response to one group's evaluations and the next group are dissatisfied and want what you had done previously!

If you are teaching on a course that goes over the academic year, a mid-year evaluation will enable you to evaluate students' progress, highlight any issues and give you time to address problems before the students complete their course. You will be seen to be doing something, but you have to be realistic with mid-year evaluations and determine what can and cannot be changed. A lot of students focus their dissatisfaction on the way the timetable is organized or the choices available to them – and sometimes these things are out of your control to change mid-year. If a particular tutor is the subject of evaluation because of the students' dissatisfaction, you have to be honest and professional about what it is possible to do – both by them and you – in such a sensitive situation. Nevertheless, in my view, face-to-face discussions are a positive form of evaluation in which students can acquire skills of negotiation, develop an understanding of how to deal with issues tactfully, learn to settle differences responsibly and also learn to accept that sometimes you have to compromise. If you engage in informal, ongoing evaluation with your students, I bet you that the formal, form-filling evaluations at the end of the course will dramatically improve and you will get more positive feedback. When this happens you will feel enthusiastic and have more energy for responding to students and making changes that improve the quality of their experience at college.

QIA – Quality Improvement Agency for Lifelong Learning. In April 2006, the Learning and Skills Development Agency (LSDA) evolved into two separate institutions. The Learning and Skills Network (LSN) is still responsible for research and development, while the QIA has the role of commissioning quality improvement work in the Learning and Skills sector. Its Chief Executive acknowledges that most of the knowledge about how to train, teach and manage well in the FE sector is available in existing good practice in colleges. It is envisaged that the QIA will move away from a standards-based approach to quality improvement (driven by inspection regimes) to one of excellence driven by talented college management. The QIA will lead on quality improvement in the sector and new programmes and initiatives will be commissioned by the agency. So, for the first time, there will be an integrated quality improvement strategy for the whole Learning and Skills sector, with an emphasis on continuous quality improvement rather than compliance.

Questioning – enquire about something to elicit an answer.
As a lecturer, you've probably fallen into the trap of posing a question to a whole group only to be rewarded by an awkward silence. Then what do you do? Answer the question yourself! Posing a question to a whole group rarely works. It's better to direct it to one student, preferably using their name. One reason for questioning is to draw students into the group and make them think: general questions allow students to sit back and wait for someone else to respond.

Although most textbooks advise you not to use closed questions, in my view they can be a good way of encouraging shy or uncommunicative students to participate. If you tell the group you only want one-word answers, 'Yes' or 'No', it's not too daunting and your praise if they're right, and encouragement to have a guess, is a way to start a dialogue with reticent students and help them to feel confident to answer more open questions.

Questions should not be perceived by students as a threat and make them feel embarrassed or uncomfortable, but should stimulate thinking. You might not get the answer you predicted, but don't dismiss it. Use supplementary questions to support thinking – and re-thinking. Be patient and show you value their answers, and also be patient when students ask questions. It may be that the pace of the session was too fast or the information was too much for students to cope with and the questions arise as a way of dealing with their learning.

If there are problems which only affect an individual student, or you feel a group is getting bogged down with niggling questions and non-urgent matters, then say you will deal with them another time. Negotiate a better time, e.g. ask them to stay at the end of the lesson or suggest they come early to the next lesson. If you are new to teaching, or need time to prepare yourself or set up and pack away, don't commit yourself to extending lessons but use tutorial time and set aside the review time at the beginning of the next session specifically to deal with questions raised.

Quizzes and Games – Learning through entertaining activities.

Learning can be fun! If students are getting to a point in a session where they're tiring, or if they're at a point in a course where they've reached a learning plateau, then what better than to introduce a quiz or game as a diversion. Quizzes can be short, light-hearted and bring pace to what otherwise might be a tedious session. Everyone can join in and have a guess.

Don't choose games that might be patronizing or embarrassing. If you want to re-energize a group, get them to do something active – but still focused on your subject. Sticking

Post-its on a chart is like putting the tail on the donkey – the fun is seeing if you've put it in the right place. This is a good game for preparing for a project or for revision – both times when you end up telling students what to do and boring everyone in the process. A game encourages students to have a go, guess and be more spontaneous. What about using two sets of cards – one with a concept/category on and one with the definitions/pictures? These can be dealt out and students have to swap cards to get matching pairs. Everyone can participate and students find it entertaining, but are learning. If you allocate points to cards, e.g. more points for harder cards, then you can introduce a bit of competition. I know that you're not supposed to encourage competition, but that's all part of the fun in any game or quiz!

R is for . . .

Race Relations

Each lecturer has a responsibility to promote racial equality in the classroom or workshop. It is not just a matter of not discriminating against Minority Ethnics yourself, but of addressing issues of discrimination between students, by colleagues or through institutional racism. There are practical ways you can promote racial equality in your everyday role as a lecturer. To raise awareness of issues, the group can jointly devise a code of behaviour for class members in induction. If language is a barrier to joining in the group and learning, then negotiating access to language courses would be a positive move. Listening to students, and ensuring other students listen to them, and encouraging them to share information about their background acknowledges cultural difference and, at the same time, acknowledges their inclusion in the group. Organizing additional support signals that underachieving students warrant support and help. Modelling acceptable behaviour yourself is important. Not accepting offensive behaviour from others whatsoever – whether it is having a joke at someone else's expense or refusing to work with someone – and dealing with it immediately makes it explicit to your group that such actions will not be tolerated. As a lecturer, it is your responsibility to ensure that everyone in your group has an equal chance of learning. For more information, see Beulah Ainley's book in this series: *A Guide to Race Equality in FE*.

Reflection – deliberating about what you do or think.

The notion of reflective practice has become a prominent one for lecturers in FE (Moon, 2004). It almost goes without saying that lecturers are expected to reflect on their practice. The idea that professionals should review their practice, and continually develop it, is a sound one. In my experience, the trouble is that lecturers – particularly those just starting out on their career – remain focused on the problems they have encountered rather than on the successes they have achieved. They look at difficult incidents within a session or in an encounter with a student or manager, and dwell on what has gone wrong. This tendency to introspection can be demoralizing and can result in destructive self-criticism – or conversely, appointing blame to others. When your self-esteem has been dented, thinking about alternative ways of handling problematic events is not easy.

If your confidence is shaken by a traumatic incident, deliberating about it on your own does not usually help matters. Of course, we can all learn from our own mistakes, but if you are feeling vulnerable it is difficult to be rational and to come up with realistic solutions to try out. There is a viewpoint, derived from Dewey (1933), that we learn most from our problems and when we have doubts about what we do. However, you may not want to risk revealing your mistakes, problems or doubts to others and expose your vulnerability by discussing them with colleagues. Despite this, sharing concerns with colleagues and confronting your problems with others who may have experienced similar situations and are empathetic is probably the best way of approaching reflective practice. Your practice is formed through your experiences. Articulating the problem, and explaining why it caused you concern, helps you to become conscious of the issues and, importantly, your reaction to them.

If you listen to the way you account for and reflect on an incident, as well as listen to your colleague's response, then you learn a great deal about yourself and your practice. Your account will almost inevitably reveal your assumptions about teaching and learning and your values and vision for education. Thus, accounts reveal the gap between what we think we should be doing and what we are doing. In this way theories and models encountered in formal study, say when undertaking your teaching qualification, are informed by the reality of classroom practice. However, what you learn from experience stands little chance of developing into good practice if you do not critically reflect on it and examine it through conversations and discussions with more experienced and supportive colleagues. Through learning conversations such as these you can make sense of your practice and formulate ways of trying out new things in future.

You cannot change the world through reflection – or even perhaps change your college systems! Neither does reflection ensure that your practice will change. What you will achieve is a more developed and informed view about what you do than you had before thinking reflectively. When you reflect on students' evaluations of teaching and learning, remember that they could have been written on a whim and are sometimes not the considered feelings and thoughts that you construe them to be. Don't be bowled over by the praise or deflated by the criticism they contain.

However, if you routinely reflect on your practice, then there is more of a chance that you will not just dwell on the problems encountered but will also establish what works well. The most valuable aspect of critical reflection is learning about yourself: your preconceptions, biases and temperament. Examining the way you really go about teaching and learning – as opposed to the way you think you ought to be going about it – is an important first step in your journey of professional development through improving practice.

Relationships

You must establish mutual trust and respect with students before you can engage in successful communication. There is no point in spending time preparing elaborate resources, researching information and having all the subject knowledge at your fingertips if you cannot communicate effectively with your students. The relationship between a lecturer and students is not intended to be one of 'friends'. The role of the lecturer is not to be a student's mate, pal or chum. Being over-familiar with students and being their buddy does not develop a positive relationship that enhances teaching and learning.

However, the relationship between a lecturer and students can be 'friendly'. Good communication is possible when you are welcoming, open, sociable, pleasant and responsive. Attending to these qualities is the key to building trust and respect. If you think about how you conduct yourself in these areas and take steps to develop these qualities in yourself, then your relationship with your students will be enhanced.

Resources – the means to aid learning.
There is a growing trend for colleges to introduce resource-based learning: and one important element is that contact time between students and a lecturer is reduced. There are good economic arguments for this but, it has to be said, not so many educational ones. In my view, the lecturer is the most important resource in the classroom. There is no doubt that you are being paid for your vocational or professional expertise and your proficiency as a teacher. The skill that you bring to the classroom encourages students to be self-directed (see more under **Zone of Proximal Development**), and it is your knowledge of your subject that enables you to support students' learning effectively, and that enable them to reach acceptable standards.

A resource that is underused is the student. Students can be a potential source of vocational expertise and up-to-date work practices. Students can use each other as a resource for information and support rather than relying solely on you. The shared experience in interaction, discussion and project work is a valuable source of learning and creates a collaborative and social learning environment.

If we take on board the latest research into learning and recognize that the individual is a 'carrier' of learning, then placing emphasis on individuals as learning resources for the whole group makes sense. For more research in FE see **Transforming Learning Cultures in FE Project**.

Review – looking back to the previous activity and looking forward to the next.

At the beginning of sessions, it is a good idea to start off by re-visiting what was done last time. Get students to sum up in a word or a phrase what the last session was about. In this way you can encourage them to identify the important skills and ideas that you introduced and talked about and gradually initiate the use and development of the skills of conceptual analysis and critical reflection appropriate to the level of the group. Reviewing at the beginning of the session also helps students to focus and settle and gives them a chance to clear up misunderstandings, or deal with anything they have been worrying about. If students missed the last session, they will not be completely lost when the new topic is introduced. However, the real importance of reviewing is to encourage students to think about the content of the last session and make connections with the current one.

If you want students to progress, you must encourage them to be actively engaged in learning in between your sessions. At the end of the session, get students to briefly review what has been covered in the current session through questions and answers. Prepare for the next session by suggesting they re-visit what has been covered today before they come next time, e.g. go over handouts, re-read any notes taken or write up notes for assessment or portfolio. Again this review can include practical things such as what to bring next time or remind students of organizational arrangements. If you are planning to use specific material next time, e.g. a handout, new vocabulary lists or a textbook chapter, give it to the students now so that they can familiarize themselves with the material before the next class, or provide them with addresses of websites they can access. Gradually, students begin to come ready for the next session, prepared to ask questions, sort out what they don't understand and make connections and links between topics in the curriculum.

With the current practice of encouraging students' learning through interaction in small groups, the reviews at the beginning and end of sessions are a way of keeping the whole group together, getting them to share ideas and experiences and encouraging them to feel part of a learning community.

S is for . . .

Scaffolding – support from those more experienced.
Bruner (1977, 1997) viewed learning as a cultural as well as a social activity, and education as a means of helping young people to negotiate meaning and create knowledge that will equip them for membership of adult society. To help this process, a more competent adult – who may be a lecturer or a peer – provides a series of prompts and questions that provokes a student to organize their experiences and thoughts and triggers growth of current skills and knowledge. Scaffolding can be used by lecturers in tutorials, seminars, coaching and question/answer sessions. Peers can use scaffolding when they are mentoring, 'buddying' or just having a conversation about their college work.

As the student gains confidence, and as they start to develop their own ideas, experiences and questions, so the support, i.e. the scaffolding, is gradually removed by the more experienced person. The aim of scaffolding is to erect it to support construction of new skills and knowledge and to slowly dismantle it as students begin to direct their own learning. For more information, see **Zone of Proximal Development**.

Session Plans – ways of organizing lessons.
The best-laid plans ... you know the adage. However well you plan, you cannot foresee everything that might happen and that might affect how your plan evolves. Session planning is no exception to this rule. I expect you've experienced this at one time or another. Your teaching room has been

changed but no one thought to tell you. Someone's moved the flipchart which you planned to use. The handout you sent for photocopying hasn't been done. The computers have just gone down. Half the students are on an educational trip with another lecturer. All these are frustrating, everyday occurrences in college which you have to cope with. Only the other day I was teaching and the classroom wall suddenly came crashing down. Well, it was a partition wall – but even so very frightening and not something you can foresee!

Notwithstanding such setbacks, lesson planning is essential so that you know what you intend to cover and how you are going to do it. You need to have some direction and structure in order to cover the criteria of your course. There is a long-standing joke in the FE sector that you only prepare session plans for teaching practice, but with the introduction of quality systems and inspection regimes this is no longer the case. Most colleges have some kind of pro-forma for you to use, which is usually designed to include all the elements that will be looked for in an inspection, including making the aim(s) of the session clear and stating the specific objective(s) of the lesson in terms of what the students will achieve and how.

However, a session plan is something you create and it doesn't have to be your master and control every minute of what you do in a lesson. It is not just about meeting inspection requirements but about your teaching and your students' learning. But, while you don't want the session plan to be too inflexible, being flexible does not mean that you abandon your plans and chat about yourself. Students like to be entertained, and you want to make the lesson interesting, but students soon complain if they don't feel they're making progress, or haven't covered enough to achieve their qualification. Being flexible means responding to students' questions, listening to their accounts of relevant workplace experience, introducing relevant items that are currently in the news or providing verbal feedback. To show that you are responding to students' needs you can incorporate time for student questions and discussion in your session plan.

It is difficult to give specific advice about the content of session plans as sessions in FE vary so much. You could be timetabled for one, two or three-hour slots, or even all day. Your session could be in a conventional classroom but it is just as likely to be in a workshop, studio, salon or laboratory. However, there are some general guidelines that would probably apply to most sessions. It is usual to outline what the session will include at the beginning of the session. Before you introduce the main topic, a good idea is to include a brief review. When you introduce the main topic make sure you link it unequivocally to the learning outcomes in your plan. Establish clear routines for the start (and end) of the session, e.g. setting up equipment; organizing the workspace safely; and using apparatus correctly. Set the standards required at the beginning of a course and gradually the students will learn what is expected of them and adopt the routines every session without you having to give constant instructions or getting annoyed when students are not ready to start the session or rush off and leave you to pack everything away. The secret is to get students actively engaged as soon as possible. This can be thinking about the topic, working things out or planning what to do – activity is not only physical.

Despite all your hard work and thinking ahead, there is a basic difficulty with session plans: students learn as individuals and you have to plan for the whole class. The dilemma is how to meet all the students' needs. As individuals they all have different experiences, abilities and motivations. If the sessions are in a 'real work environment', in a practical workshop or on a specific vocational course, then students will have individual action plans. Otherwise, the only way to address this is to ensure you have a variety of activities so that diverse learning needs or styles can be met.

Catering for differences in pace of working can be tricky. When you set a time for an activity you risk allowing too much time, and quicker students waste time. Alternatively, you allow too little time and the intended outcome of the activity is lost. You get better at timing with practice, but if you're unsure ask a more experienced colleague what they think. Recording actual times against the intended times at the end of the lesson will help you adjust the timings when you use the plan again. Keep all your session plans in clearly marked files on your computer. After each session evaluate the plan. Spending a few minutes on evaluation when the session is fresh in your memory is an excellent way of developing your skill at preparing interesting and well-paced sessions. Read more about plans under **Review**.

Skills for Life Agenda (S4L)

The key ideas incorporated in the Skills for Life (S4L) Agenda emanated from the Moser Report (1999). This report was commissioned by the government to find out the level of basic skills of adults in the UK. The results were quite shocking – 20 per cent of adults in the UK had low levels of basic skills. For these adults, this meant that they could not read simple instructions or work out simple sums. For the government, this was seen as evidence that low levels of basic skills can prevent people from being economically independent and can lead to social exclusion. It was claimed by the government that S4L would encourage adults to take basic qualifications and improve their literacy and numeracy skills as it was to be more accessible, e.g. through LearnDirect and family learning projects. What was also driving this initiative was the government's concern that Britain's prosperity is at risk because so many adults cannot read, write or add up properly.

Despite enormous amounts of money, the Adult Learners Institute (ALI) reported in 2005 that there has been a depressing lack of improvement and a failure to tackle weaknesses in literacy and numeracy over the past few years. S4L was not just directed at adults but at trainers and lecturers – and basic skills standards are now included in generic teaching standards for the FE sector. You cannot put all the blame at the door of those involved in S4L training or at FE lecturers, as the Moser Report linked the low levels of basic skills to several factors: poverty, bad health, inadequate housing and unemployment. Tackling low levels of literacy and numeracy must be part of tackling wider economic and social issues.

SOLO Taxonomy – Structure of Observed Learning Outcomes.

A taxonomy is a classification of information and the SOLO taxonomy (Biggs, 1999) is a developmental schema that describes how the way students represent their learning (e.g. how they organize their assessments or structure their projects and portfolios) and reveals what stage they are in their understanding as they make sense of a subject. It is claimed that the SOLO taxonomy can be applied to any subject area, but works best for academic subjects. However, I've found it useful to refer to when assessing vocational and professional qualifications.

The first stage in the taxonomy is called 'prestructural' and describes how students can acquire information in your sessions (or in the workplace) and make no real sense of it. An example which illustrates this lack of structure clearly is when a student comes to a portfolio workshop or tutorial and presents you with a pile of documents, notes, records, witness statements, photographs, etc., in no particular order, which they have accumulated. They tell you that they have been really busy and collected loads of stuff and they've even more of it on the computer. But, when you ask them what unit it relates to or what criteria it covers they shuffle the pile around as they try to make sense of it – but have little idea. Quantity does not make for quality and you know the student does not really understand what is required.

The next level of structure is called 'unistructural', which focuses on one aspect well enough but without identifying its significance. To continue with the same example, a student may have completed one section of a portfolio but has no idea if the evidence is adequate or can be cross-referenced.

When you get to the next level, which is 'multistructural', you can find several relevant aspects in, say, an essay or report, but they don't hang together at all. They are just written up as they are thought about, in no particular order and with no recognizable logic.

When students link together their ideas and make sense of the different aspects, e.g. draw conclusions from them, you can say their learning is at the 'relational' level in the SOLO

taxonomy. Students can justify why they've included something and how it contributes to the whole piece.

The next stage is when a student can do all these things
and then go on to extend their ideas to a new area, e.g. a
practitioner doing a project in Early Years Education not only
identifies good classroom practice but extends the findings
into the field of Professional Development by developing a
framework that other practitioners might consider adopting.
In this example, at the 'extended abstract' level, the practitioner has extrapolated what they have learned in one setting
and applied it to develop more general guidelines to consider
and judge whether they may be of use in other settings.

The SOLO taxonomy can be very useful when discussing
students' progress in tutorials or when assessing their learning. It's well worth a try! These ideas link to **Deep Learning**.

T is for . . .

Teaching Qualifications – Qualified Teacher Learning and Skills.

A new teaching qualification called Qualified Teacher Learning and Skills (QTLS) is at the centre of reforms for the training of teachers in the Learning and Skills Sector, including FE lecturers (DfES, 2004). The policy enshrines the expectation that all students will be taught by qualified and skilled lecturers. The teaching qualification will be introduced in full in 2007. Lecturers have a wide range of specialist teaching areas, roles and responsibilities and this is recognized by the provision of subject-specific mentors and coaches. There are two stages: the Passport to Teaching Award, which everyone has to achieve, and the QTLS Licence to Practise, which is the full qualification and compulsory for full-time, part-time and fractional teachers.

For the first time there is a Continuing Professional Development Phase, which is part of the requirement to maintain a licence to practise. QTLS can be achieved via this route by those who exited following the Passport to Teaching Award. These reforms are far-reaching and will mean changes in practice and culture for employers, individual teachers and for those who train them according to Standards Unit. For further details, send off for the DfES publication *ITT Reform 1*.

Teaching Style – your personal approach to teaching.

It seems to me that people talk a great deal about learning styles but less about teaching styles. Why is that? Do you have a preferred teaching style, in the same way as students are said to have a preferred or dominant learning style? Have you ever tried to identify your teaching style or assess how effective it is? Dixon and Woolhouse (1996) devised a questionnaire to assess your preferred teaching style, based on the learning style questionnaire developed by Honey and Mumford (1986). Dixon and Woolhouse suggest that you are often unaware of your 'inclinations' to a particular way of teaching, e.g. do you know if you are you an activist, reflector, theorist or pragmatist teacher? Completing the questionnaire puts you in a better position to select teaching methods that broaden your teaching style.

Among the teaching styles that were admired not all that long ago – and which lecturers were taught to emulate – were being a skilled instructor, a good disciplinarian, an adept public speaker and an entertaining performer. Taking charge, dictating notes, giving instructions and keeping students quiet were all fundamental to being a good teacher in FE. A sense of humour was an asset that helped you get through a class as students were busy practising and drilling their skills, copying up notes, revising or doing tests. Then, the important features of good practice were for the teacher to have control of the lesson content, the pace of delivery, the structure of the session and the expected outcomes.

These attributes are no longer considered appropriate when you are trying to encourage student autonomy. Given the promotion of student-centred learning and its increased acceptance in recent years, the teaching styles that are regarded as good practice today are not the same as they were yesterday. It is no longer enough to focus on your teaching; you have to focus on students' learning. If you look at your teaching from this perspective, then the styles you can adopt to encourage autonomy become apparent as the balance of control changes.

The teaching style that most of you will be familiar with is that of facilitator, i.e. someone who is a catalyst for students' learning (Rogers, 1983). It is imperative to remember that you cannot make students learn. You can only provide an environment which is conducive to learning. It is critical to remember that learning is not a product of teacher activity.

What *you* do is under your *direct* control, not what the students do. However, your activities, e.g. ensuring a supportive and encouraging environment, facilitate the necessary conditions for your students' learning.

A variation of this teaching style is that of the co-constructor. Barth (2000) advises the use of this style, as she believes that constructing knowledge is not something that students do spontaneously and so requires negotiation. The construction of new knowledge is thus a shared responsibility, and this teaching style requires lecturers to display good interpersonal communication skills with students.

Many lecturers in FE take on the teaching style of guru. They have been appointed as an expert in their subject and it is this expertise that gives them authority in the classroom. Students take their lead from self-styled gurus, but are often a bit in awe of them and reluctant to challenge anything they say. If you take on the teaching style of a guide, rather than a guru, you still use your expert knowledge: but rather than providing all the information and advice, you steer the students in the right direction as and when they require it, and point out the way that will lead to success (Freeman, 2003). The teaching style of a guide is more about showing students the way than telling them, and so the students have to do the work themselves.

Eisner (2004) suggests that the form of thinking needed by artists to create artistically crafted work is also needed by lecturers to be effective. The artist has to be imaginative and resourceful in handling materials and creating an innovative end product – all things the lecturer has to do when supporting students' learning. You may not always exhibit the dexterity of the artist – and sometimes when working with students you may feel more like a sculptor hewing marble than a potter shaping malleable clay – but the end product will be worth it!

It is evident that to support student autonomy, any teaching style adopted must gradually pass control to the students so that they progressively have the freedom to direct their own learning. The teaching styles that are admired today are being an approachable tutor, an empathetic coach and a wise mentor. Developing a rapport with students, providing choice, acknowledging diversity and advocating inclusive activities are all considered fundamental to being a good teacher in FE today. Whatever teaching style you adopt, it should not only make use of your own strengths but also encompass these features.

Timetables – documents used to calculate hours and allocate classes.

Timetables structure individual and college life – but are everyday documents that are taken for granted. They identify subjects, their level and the nature of the groups being taught. However, as documents they do little to reveal the pressures and fragmentation of a lecturer's workload. The way timetables are constructed may actually contribute to a lecturer's workload. What is visible on the timetable relates to the teaching commitment, as only the hours in the classroom are shown. What is invisible is group size, the number and type of assessments, and the nature of the students. What appears to be problematic for lecturers is therefore what we cannot see on the timetable: the administrative burdens, frequent meetings, increasing student demands, tight deadlines and constant curriculum change.

My contention is that these factors, along with the way teaching is allocated and organized, hold hidden pressures and increase a lecturer's workload. A timetable is a poor indicator of a lecturer's daily routine in that a great deal of what is accomplished does not appear on it. The time spent on non-teaching activities could be limitless and a lecturer's day is regularly extended by working through lunch and tea breaks or taking work home. Non-teaching time is required for the development of innovative new courses and creating quality resources, but lecturers are being required to undertake more administrative tasks. Much of what is undertaken is not recorded or recognized – it is invisible and so is not readily addressed by those responsible for timetabling or by college managers.

Transforming Learning Cultures in FE Project

You probably think of TLC as 'tender loving care' – but in fact the TLC Project investigated learning in 17 sites across four partner FE colleges in different parts of England over a three-year period (between 2001 and 2004), and reported in November, 2005. In all, over 600 interviews were transcribed and analysed, 150 observations recorded and 1,043 questionnaires returned and analysed. The research was conducted as a partnership between HE and FE and was the largest, most rigorous and most in-depth investigation of learning in the UK FE sector that has yet been completed.

The TLC Project identified pressures that threaten the quality of learning in FE, developed a better way to understand learning in FE, and produced a new multi-level approach to improving learning in FE. This approach derived from the fact that so many factors influence learning in FE, e.g. disposition of students and lecturers, location and resources of the college and its management, assessment specifications, timetables, funding and inspection regimes, government policy and broader social values and practices, etc. You can see why the researchers came up with the term 'culture' to define the practices which influence learning in FE, rather than keep referring to the countless factors involved.

Four key features were identified within learning cultures: the central significance of the tutor in learning; the comparatively low status of the sector that offers a second chance in education; inadequate and unstable funding and rigid inspection; and the demand that the FE sector provides effective responses to some of the country's major social, employment and economic needs.

Part of the Project was to bring about change in the learning culture, and three types of intervention were distinguished: interventions for improvement, i.e. to foster better learning and maximize student success; interventions to mitigate change, i.e. maintaining professional practices in conflict with new management expectations; and interventions for 'exit', i.e. some tutors left the FE sector.

The TLC Project identified four possible drivers for improvement of learning: student interests; tutor professionalism; pedagogy; and a cultural view of learning. The Project set out six broad principles – which could underpin nationally established principles of procedure – setting out approaches to improving learning, rather than rely on measured outputs. This is essential reading for all FE lecturers and the TLC project website has all the details: www.education.ex.ac.uk/tlc.

U is for . . .

Uncertainty

If there is one thing you can be certain about, it is that uncertainty pervades the FE sector! You cannot remove it from life in the FE sector and it appears inherent throughout the education system. It is inescapable as new initiatives and policies are introduced and implemented one after the other in quick succession. Professional work is characterized by unpredictability and the role of the lecturer is no exception. We can't re-write the rules, alter the speed at which new initiatives are introduced or maintain the status quo. What we can do as lecturers is learn how to anticipate change a bit more and plan its implementation in a more informed way, and not react immediately to every new initiative and edict.

We can deal with uncertainty by developing college strategies and identifying priorities. This requires collaborative working with colleagues and it is through sharing everyday events like course evaluation, facing the ups and downs of college funding, admitting mistakes in target setting and facing disappointments about staffing and resources that we learn what it is that drives change in college. When our conversations with colleagues focus on everyday events that create uncertainty, it gives everyone a reason to engage in professional learning and work collaboratively at planning change; otherwise all you can do is bemoan your situation.

Union Learning Representatives (ULRs)

Another acronym to add to your list! In 2005 the National Association of Teachers in Further and Higher Education (which became the University and College Union in June 2006) introduced into colleges a new concept of Union Learning Representatives (ULRs), who are trained to provide professional development opportunities for lecturers. This concept has worked successfully in industry but it is the first time that such an initiative has been introduced in colleges.

The areas of immediate concern for the ULRs in FE are initial teacher training and continuing professional development (as Lifelong Learning UK has set targets for all full-time and part-time lecturers to have acquired Qualified Teacher Learning and Skills status, and continuing professional development is now part of a requirement to maintain licence to practise) and teaching 14–16 year olds (whom lecturers have not been trained to teach).

ULRs will work with colleges towards equitable distribution of professional development within and across colleges. Initially the ULRs see their role as lessening the stress of lecturers' working lives and letting them be honest about their level of skills, which they probably don't want to reveal to managers. One new ULR sent out an intranet survey to 170 branch members about their training needs and the results revealed requests for stress-relieving courses such as massage, meditation, music and gardening. Sounds just what we all need! For more information ask your UCU college representative.

Using Practitioner Research – enquiring into your own practice.

Stenhouse (1975) recognized teachers as researchers and advocated that the best way of developing as a professional is constantly to question your practice. I am sure that many of you do question what you do all the time, but I wonder how many of you systematically plan a research project on a particular aspect of your practice that you wish to change or improve? Not very many, I suspect.

However, if you face curriculum or organizational problems in your daily work, then you may benefit from undertaking small-scale research. The closer the research focus is to your everyday workplace practice, the more manageable it will be to undertake. The benefits accrue from actually undertaking the research, working collaboratively with colleagues and generating evidence to present to managers to support requests to implement change.

Although researching practice is linked to the notion of reflective practice, it is more than reflection. If you are aiming at improving some aspect of teaching and learning, you need to clearly identify the problem that concerns you, consider the issues and consult colleagues or team members before planning any change. There is criticism of small-scale research as it only applies to your research setting, e.g. a Diploma in Music, and is not applicable across similar courses across the college, let alone the sector. Notwithstanding such criticisms, if you are rigorous as a researcher, your results may interest others involved in your specialist area and it is up to them to test your results, find out what is happening in their setting and see if your findings stand up.

Jameson and Hillier (2003) argue that because the FE sector is so complex and lecturers are required to implement change so rapidly, they need to investigate their own practices. They urge lecturers to start in a small way through the use of research into their own practice, and use evidence to further test out ideas in other situations. Read *Researching Post-Compulsory Education* (Jameson and Hillier, 2003) for practical ideas on how you can make a difference.

Using other people's research is another good way of improving your own practice and keeping up to date. You are probably aware of journals that publish research in your subject or curriculum area. However, there are three academic journals that are pertinent to lecturers in FE that contain articles by academics and practitioners about teaching and learning in the FE sector, and are an excellent way of finding out about what is going on in the research community. The journals are the *Journal of Further and Higher Education*, the *Journal of Vocational Education and Training* and *Research in Post Compulsory Education*. Your college probably has subscriptions to these journals, and if so you can access them on the internet or read printed versions if they are kept in the library.

V is for ...

Verification – confirmation of good practice and procedures.

Verification is to ensure all candidates have access to fair and reliable assessment. If you are a lecturer or assessor on any National Vocational Qualification course, then you will need to conform to a system of recording students' progress and achievement to satisfy the awarding body. All your records and a sample of your marked work will be checked by a colleague acting as an internal verifier. The internal verifier should brief all assessors about the process and ensure they are properly trained and suitably qualified. Their role is to check that you are acting consistently and appropriately as an assessor, and that your records are accurate and authentic.

The quality assurance procedures are then subject to external verification. An external verifier checks that assessment procedures meet the regulations of the awarding body and ensures local standards match national standards. The external verifier can be an excellent source of advice and guidance about good practice in delivering and assessing your National Vocational Qualification.

Visual, Auditory and Kinaesthetic (VAK)

A strategy engaging the whole brain in learning – not just one side or the other – is a response to recent studies about the structure and workings of the human brain (Smith, 1998). The brain has two distinct sides and each is responsible for different things. The left cerebral hemisphere of the brain is often thought of as the logical, thinking side. Speech is controlled by the left side and left-brain dominant students are usually good at reasoning, the use of language and number skills. Left-brain dominant students are said to prefer structure and organization, and are usually attentive and realistic.

The right cerebral hemisphere of the brain is thought of as the creative, imaginative side. Spatial imagery and athleticism are controlled by the right side of the brain. When a student is right-brain dominant they are said to exhibit characteristics such as being sporty, liking to work in groups, and enjoying drawing and singing. Such students prefer visual instructions and are not so good at listening to verbal explanations, remembering facts or dealing with numbers. Right-brain dominant students are described as spontaneous and enjoy creative arts and music.

So, engaging the whole brain in learning is intended to integrate these characteristics and qualities. How does this work in practice? It is suggested that 29 per cent of us are Visual learners, 34 per cent of us are Auditory learners and 37 per cent of us are Kinaesthetic learners. Although this is a contentious idea to many educational researchers, what it means in practice is that teaching is not just about covering the curriculum content. Teaching has to appeal to all our senses and so must be varied, and as a result traditional 'talk and chalk' teaching has been abandoned in favour of creating a positive learning environment where students are taught in ways that 'engage' them and that meet their individual learning styles. Teaching methods and resources have to cater for the different learning styles and needs of Visual, Auditory and Kinaesthetic learners. This means recognizing and valuing the differences between students, and responding to those differences by planning balanced sessions that take into account what might affect learning positively or negatively for each student. To enable students to develop as independent thinkers and active learners, emphasis is placed on self-management and study skills. This is supported by providing positive feedback and stimulating advice and by helping students to set personal goals. Evaluation of these goals is then used to inform future teaching.

Although acknowledgement of Visual, Auditory and Kinaesthetic learners and their different learning styles is common in primary and secondary schools, it is less prevalent in FE teaching and learning. Despite controversy surrounding the ideas that healthy brains make healthy learners, there are some important aspects of this approach to teaching and learning that FE lecturers could profit from. There is a belief that every learner can improve and that you have to look for a student's strengths and focus on everyday successes and take pride in them. Considering approaches that recognize Visual, Auditory and Kinaesthetic learners raises awareness of important factors that could inhibit learning, e.g. a student's poor sight, hearing loss or attention deficit. As well as promoting brain exercises, this approach also stresses that brains don't function well for long periods and students therefore need frequent breaks as concentration lapses. The body doesn't function well when dehydrated and so it is advocated that students drink plenty of water during sessions.

Brain-based learning consists of a range of techniques that deem learning to be fun and that are said to boost motivation, attention-span, understanding and recall. If you have students who are frustrated by failure, struggling to keep up or don't seem to have any goals, then perhaps it would be worthwhile thinking about whether they are Visual, Auditory or Kinaesthetic learners and incorporating some of these ideas into your sessions. After all, variety is the spice of life! For more information, see **Accelerated Learning**.

Vocational excellence – recognition of quality provision. Centre of Vocational Excellence (CoVE) status is awarded to providers of vocational training who have demonstrated success at Level 3 in meeting a skills priority, whether locally, regionally or nationally. To achieve CoVE status, FE colleges and other providers must have demonstrated good practice in vocational training through inspection (or other forms of external accreditation). One of the aspects involved in achieving special CoVE status is a commitment to sharing good practice and funding to enable this. Staff in a CoVE are expected to attend development groups to facilitate sharing good practice within colleges, and a percentage of funding awarded because of CoVE status must be spent on dissemination activities between providers of vocational training. This could be, for example, sharing good practice in assessment and verification procedures with NVQ assessors and verifiers in other vocational areas across a college, or with other training providers.

Voice – used to communicate with students.
As lecturers use their voice so much in teaching in FE, it is not surprising how often you find lecturers suffering from sore throats, croaky voices, or sometimes even losing their voice. The voice is sensitive to tensions in the body and when you are ill at ease or stressed out you become susceptible to aches and pains, and it is often the throat and voice that suffer. If colds and 'flu are going around you're bound to pick them up in a hot, stuffy classroom or a cold, draughty workshop!

It is natural to be nervous on occasions, but you can't make the best of yourself when you're tense, your voice is hoarse and wavers and it hurts to talk. The best cure is to talk less and certainly not to raise your voice or shout. What I do if I have a sore throat is to suck a sweet, drink plenty of water and keep quiet! The reason for this is that your voice and you are one, so if you're feeling down and under the weather that's how you come across. You don't want to send out signals to students that you can't be bothered with them.

If you're a compulsive talker – and many of us are – losing your voice should raise your awareness of how much you talk in a session and probably how little the students do. So, if you're feeling sorry for yourself, nursing a cold and have a sore throat, remember it's not the end of the world and could be the time to make a resolution to talk less and listen more: less teacher talk and more student activity. It's not just good practice, but your voice is an essential resource and you need to take care of it.

W is for . . .

Women and Work – job segregation in the workplace.
Gender divisions are prevalent in the workplace and job segregation is common. What we are talking about in job segregation is the criticism that students are steered into jobs on the basis of gender as a result of careers guidance in school, college or at Job Centres. Females tend to be steered into traditional jobs in areas of employment such as caring, catering and clerical work. Males also tend to end up in conventional areas of employment such as engineering or construction. Job segregation between males and females may seem to you to be something that is beyond your power to do anything about, but is that really the case?

The Women and Work Commission, set up by the government to tackle the pay gap between the sexes, revealed that many women are trapped in low-paid jobs because they are not given other options while still in education. The education system seems to fail women at the points where choices about possible future employment are discussed and made. In tutorials, do you encourage female students to be aspirational and discuss less traditional job opportunities or different training and educational opportunities? Of course, there are females on engineering and construction courses – but the numbers are derisory. Female students really are the exception to the rule on such courses.

The government's concern naturally focuses on economic as much as gender issues. Inequality is costing the economy billions of pounds a year. Shortages of skilled women in sectors such as IT and construction mean a real loss in national productivity. So, perhaps colleges can do more to

address issues of women and work and to encourage female students to obtain skills in areas of shortage. It goes without saying that this also applies to the inclusion of men in more 'female-dominated' work roles, such as nursing and primary school teaching.

Wording Assignments – composing fair assessment. Students complain that they could have got better marks in an assignment if they'd known what was required! It's not necessarily that they've been absent or haven't made progress and can't make sense of your subject; it could be that the way the assignment was written didn't make it clear exactly what was required. You usually realize this only when it's too late – probably when giving feedback to a disappointed student.

In order to ensure that an assignment is clear to students, you need to go through the requirements in detail in class. If it is evident that they don't understand or are confused about a particular instruction or section, then you need to consider changing the wording. If you do this in discussion with students, you will be sure that you've addressed the problem revealed in the original writing of the assignment.

Writing assignments needs care and improves with practice. Don't chuck out an assignment just because one section didn't work. In FE we don't get the chance to trial assignments or pilot them before use, so make adjustments to assignments each time you use them and you will end up with ones that are clear to students and cover the criteria.

Working in Groups – learning in the company of peers. Ironically, becoming an independent learner can be achieved through working in groups with other course members. If students are to move towards autonomy, then they need a context in which to develop independence. When students start a new course there is a tendency to exhibit dependent behaviour. As a lecturer, you might observe some students are inhibited; they show lack of commitment to participate and little communication with you or other course members.

To enable a shift from dependence on the lecturer as an authority figure and a source of information, students need experiences of carrying out tasks and activities (and coping with the problems they pose) without constantly seeking the lecturer's help and reassurance. Students become more independent as learners through working with and helping each other. Learning occurs through interaction between group members and the consideration of different points of view within the group. Working in groups, therefore, is the context that provides opportunities for students to experience these interactions.

Working with others in a group, and resolving issues together, provides a safe environment in which students can develop a sense of themselves as individuals who are capable of acting and thinking independently. Group work also provides an opportunity for students to realize that they can't just take from the group; to benefit, they have to contribute to it as well.

When students are working in groups, different skills from those used in class teaching are demanded from the lecturer. The lecturer acts as a facilitator more than an instructor or teacher. Initially, groups often don't work very long before they initiate contact with the lecturer. In my experience, these are usually questions about how to proceed, how you want the task done, how long they have, etc. Student-initiated contacts can be lessened by good planning, organization and instructions – as can 'inactive' time when some groups are waiting for others to finish.

Lecturer-initiated contacts can be limited to ensuring students are still on task, checking progress, and motivating groups if they are flagging or falling out. Groups have the potential to provide opportunities for students not merely to engage in discussion but also to create a social 'family' to which they can belong and identify with – but groups, just like families, can also be a source of frustration, despite the best intentions (Jacques, 2000). However, you can create the climate in which students can become successful at working independently from you in groups – after all, they have the support of others in the group. If you organize group work to help students towards autonomy, resist interrupting and don't keep tabs on their activities every other second! To help students become independent learners, as a lecturer you have to let students make more and more decisions about learning as the course proceeds. It's tough, I know, but what this means is that you're not constantly needed by your students and are no longer the centre of attention!

X is for . . .

Xtra Support – additional learning support.
There could be a whole range of factors that constrain students from being successful on the course they've enrolled on and that stop them from gaining the qualifications they set out to achieve. If you have a large group, it is not always easy to give each student the extra support they need. Obviously, as a personal tutor you try to do your best for all your students and as a course tutor you are keen that students succeed and don't drop out for their own sake – not just because of your concerns about retention and achievement.

When you're stretched and overloaded, your students don't get the best deal and you need to find extra support for them elsewhere. You can't provide everything for students yourself and this means that you'll need to work with colleagues across college to get students the additional support they need. Your students may need help with their spelling or numeracy skills. You can refer students for additional help, which is probably one-to-one and addresses what they need. Colleges provide special areas – sometimes in a library or an IT centre – where students can access help from staff with specialized training and knowledge. This is brilliant for students with dyslexia, learning impairments or just lack of confidence in their ability. Many colleges have a system of student mentoring or buddying and this is a great source of extra help, so it's worth investigating whether your students could benefit from such a scheme.

Students do not neatly fall into one category, and it may be that you refer students to a college counsellor for additional support. They might benefit from language lessons if English

is their second language. You could also refer students for guidance in financial matters, e.g. on the maintenance allowance, or for help with sorting out accommodation. All these factors impact on students' learning and if your college can provide extra support, you'll have a lot more happy customers. You may not be able to personally provide the extra support for students that they need, and you don't have to be the only source of support for students and work yourself into the ground. You have plenty of colleagues across college who are there to provide extra support, so get them involved in supporting your students as this also provides extra support for you!

Y is for . . .

You – a tutor in the FE sector.

At last there is real evidence that *you* matter. The latest research in the FE sector (TLC Project, 2006) identified that a key feature of learning cultures in FE is the central significance of the tutor in learning. *You* are important! Your expertise and actions are important in enhancing and sustaining learning.

Over the years, there have been repeated calls for the improvement of teaching and learning. What the research identifies is that these pressures are driven by concerns other than the nature of teaching and learning. It is the demand for the sector to provide effective responses to some of the country's major social, employment and economic needs – and with ever-decreasing resources – that puts *you* in the front line.

An important role identified for *you* is to mediate the aspects of a learning culture that you can influence. For example: How do *you* overcome dramatic reductions in class contact time? How do *you* manage the tensions between inclusion and high achievement rates? Obviously individual lecturers differ, and there are variations across the sector, but this frequently entails large amounts of what the researchers define as 'underground' working, whereby tutors routinely engage in working well beyond their job descriptions.

Working in this way may sap your energy and lower morale – but *you* do it for the students: that's what gives *you* job satisfaction.

Young Learners – 14 to 16 year olds.

When you've been teaching in the FE sector for as many years as I have, practically all students appear to come under the category of young learners! What policy-makers and lecturers are referring to when they use the term is students aged 14 to 16, now that *is* young! If you mention this group of learners to colleagues in college, more often than not the response is raised eyebrows – at the least.

Including 14 to 16 year olds as part of the college community has been problematic in many respects, but the problems are far from new. Colleges have always been involved with young learners through 'school-link' schemes, etc. As evidence of this, I quote the textbook I used when studying for my teaching qualifications, which states that increasing the numbers of young learners in FE: '...will present the colleges with many problems, ranging from the extended provision of facilities to the winning over of large numbers of young persons to the view that continued education is to their advantage' (Curzon, 1976: 205). What comes around goes around.

It is the White Paper, *14–19 Education and Skills* (DfES, 2005), that sets out changes to the structure of education and qualifications for young learners. It advocates stronger vocational routes and greater choice of subjects and modes of study, particularly to motivate those who are in danger of dropping out of education. The biggest change is that 14 to 16 year olds who do not wish to pursue academic study but to work instead remain on their own school roll but can access other schools, colleges or training providers for vocationally-based courses. Statutory requirements for school attendance are waived for part of the week. In school, those who elect for this different route pursue the Key Stage 4 National Curriculum core and foundation subjects. In other settings, they pursue a work-focused programme with an emphasis on vocational development and experience, personal and social development and a catch-up on basic and Key Skills.

The current reforms are linked to long-term government targets for increasing participation in post-16 education. There is a realization that if targets were to be achieved for young people staying in education and training post-16 – such as increasing the number of young people participating in education at 17 from 75% now to 90% by 2015 – then there is a need to tackle the problem of disengagement before that age.

Although lecturers applaud the motives behind re-engagement programmes for 14 to 16 year olds, because they are aimed at young learners who are lower achieving, at risk of truanting or non-attendance, they do present them with a dilemma. They are the ones trying to persuade young learners to re-engage, and this is not easy or straightforward. Eliciting the reasons why this cohort of 14 to 16 year olds wish to engage in learning is proving a hard task. You are not alone if you are at a loss as to what to do and feel like tearing your hair out. Just read this: 'Issues of motivation, disruptive learners and simply dealing with young adolescents require professional development and experience and many of you ... will be only too well aware of the demands being placed on you by dealing with this new group of learners' (Hillier, 2005: 45).

All these changes impact on lecturers who entered the FE sector to teach the post-16s. However much you want to help young learners who have not achieved in school, just dealing with adolescents is a challenge. Finding ways of working with this age group is a big learning curve. Some help is at hand. A *Manual of Good Practice* can be accessed on the DfES website: www.dfes.gov.uk/14-19/. Alternatively, you can order a hard copy online at: www.dfes.gov.uk/publications (DfES Ref: 2103-2005DOC-EN). The LSDA has developed *Guidance for FE Colleges Providing for Young Learners* and other resources: look at the website for up-to-date information: www.vocationallearning.org.uk.

Z is for ...

Zone of Proximal Development – potential between present development level and developmental level one is able to reach through interaction with others.

This all sound a bit of a mouthful, and it doesn't help that the person whose idea it is was called Vygotsky! Vygotsky (1962) claims that an individual's ability to think and reason by themselves is a result of activities mediated by language in social interactions. The theory is that we use language not just to communicate with others, but also for dialogue with ourselves, i.e. in our thinking. This is how we acquire new understandings, interpretations and insights.

So, what Vygotsky is saying is that an individual's progress and learning is developed through social interaction. This can be with parents, schoolteachers, lecturers, colleagues or employers. At first, an individual constructs meanings from understanding the language used by others. Next, they depend on others to nurture and support their efforts. Then, they rely on others to introduce them to new ways of thinking and acting.

Vygotsky felt that the way children mastered something they couldn't do before was the key to successful learning – not just in childhood but throughout life. If we apply this to the FE sector, it means that students can achieve more with assistance than they can alone. For example, through interaction with others in, say, tutorials, groupwork and discussions, students can be made aware of *new* ideas and link them with their existing ideas. The important thing is that they can't do this on their own – they can only do this with the help of (and experience of) interaction with others. Activities beyond a student's current capabilities require the assistance of a more capable and competent 'other' (whether it be lecturer, peer or employer) to help bridge the gap between what could be achieved on their own and what can be achieved with the support and help of others.

To facilitate learning in this way, see **Scaffolding**.

Zzz ... – the sound of someone snoozing.

Imagine the scene, your class starts at 6 pm and doesn't finish until 9 pm. According to the weathergirl, it's been the hottest day of the year so far. Students start arriving. Some have driven 30 miles or more, after a full day's work. You make a start on the session. Someone opens the window wider and you prop open the door to create a draught. You've got to get on because it's the last session before the exam and there's so much to do. Just as you're about to suggest a little break you notice that someone's eyes are closed – they've dozed off!

Did you drone on so much that they couldn't take any more? More likely, the combination of listening to you, feeling tired after work, rushing to class and the heat all took their toll. We've all experienced this in a boring film, play or sermon. You feel your eyelids getting heavy and then ...well, you don't feel anything as you've dozed off! Usually you wake up pretty quickly, feeling groggy and embarrassed.

So, don't make fun of the student or make a joke of the situation. Try to put yourself in their position and deal with it sensitively. Be aware of their feelings. Get another member of the class to speak to them rather than do it yourself and so enable them to save face. Situations like this make you realize just how much effort students make to get to your sessions, let alone the effort required to do all the studying. How do you think the students would react if the tables were turned? Now a real problem might be if the zzz ... was coming from you!

References

Barth, B.-M. (2000). 'The teachers' construction of knowledge', in B. Moon, J. Butcher and E. Bird (eds), *Leading Professional Development in Education*. London: Routledge Falmer/OUP.

Biggs, J. (1999). *Teaching for Quality Learning in Higher Education*. Buckingham: SRHE/Open University Press.

Bolton, G. (2001). *Reflective Practice: Writing and Professional Development*. Paul Chapman: London.

Bruner, J. (1977). *The Process of Education*. New York: John Wiley.

Bruner, J. (1986). *Actual Minds, Possible Worlds*. Cambridge, MA: Harvard University Press.

Bruner, J. (1990). *Acts of Meaning*. Cambridge, MA: Harvard University Press.

Bruner, J. (1997). *The Culture of Education*. Cambridge, MA: Harvard University Press.

Curzon, L. (1976). *Teaching in Further Education: An outline of principles and practice*. London: Cassell.

Daniels, H. (2001). *Vygotsky and Pedagogy*. Routledge Falmer: London.

Dearing, R. (1996). Review of Qualifications for 16–19 Year Olds (Dearing II). Hayes: SCAA.

Department for Education and Skills (2004). *Equipping Our Teachers for the Future: Reforming initial teacher training for the learning and skills sector*. www.dfes.gov.uk.

Department for Education and Skills (2005). *14–19 Education and Skills*. www.dfes.gov.uk.

Department for Education and Skills (2005). *Reducing Re-Offending through Skills and Employment*. www.dfes.gov.uk.

Department for Education and Skills (2006). *Education and Inspections Bill*. www.dfes.gov.uk.

Dewey, J. (1933). *How We Think: A restatement of the relation of reflective thinking in the educative process.* Chicago: Henry Regnery.

Dixon, T. and Woolhouse, M. (1996). 'The relationship between teachers' and learners' teaching and learning styles', in *Journal of Further and Higher Education,* 20(3), Autumn, pp. 15–22.

Dunn, P. and Finnemore, C. (2004). *Attitudinal Based Learning: Giving learners the choices they need.* www.p3t.com.

Eisner, E. (1991). *The Enlightened Eye: Qualitative inquiry and the enhancement of educational practice.* New York: Macmillan

Eisner, E. (2004). 'What Can Education Learn from the Arts about the Practice of Education?', in *International Journal of Education and the Arts,* 5(4), pp. 1–12

Elliott, J. (1991). *Action Research for Educational Change.* Buckingham: OUP.

Eraut, M. (1994). *Developing Professional Knowledge and Competence.* London: Falmer Press.

Fillingham, L. (1993). *Foucault for Beginners.* Writers and Readers Books: New York.

Foster, A. (2005). *Realising the Potential: A review of the future role of further education colleges.* www.dfes.gov.uk/furthereducation/fereview.

Freeman, J. (2003). 'Suffering from Certainty', in *Research in Post-compulsory Education,* 8(1), pp. 39–52.

Gardner, H. (1983). *Frames of Mind.* New York: Basic Books

Gardner, H. (1999). *Reframed: Multiple intelligences for the 21st century.* New York: Basic Books.

Goleman, D. (1995). *Emotional Intelligence: Why it can matter more than IQ.* London: Bloomsbury Publishing.

Goleman, D. (1998). *Working with Emotional Intelligence.* London: Bloomsbury Publishing.

Green, M. (2002). *Improving One-to-one Tutorials.* London: LSDA

Hanson, A. (1996). 'The search for a separate theory of adult learning: Does anyone really need andragogy?', in R. Edwards, A. Hanson and P. Raggatt (eds) *Boundaries of Adult Learning.* London: Routledge/Open University Press.

Hillier, Y. (2005). *Reflective Teaching in Further and Adult Education* (2nd edn), London: Continuum.

Hoban, G. (2002). *Teacher Learning for Educational Change*. Buckingham: Open University Press.

Honey, P. and Mumford, A. (1986). *A Manual of Learning Styles*. Maidenhead: Peter Honey.

Jacques, D. (2000). *Learning in Groups* (3rd edn). London: Kogan Page.

Jameson, J. and Hillier, Y. (2003). *Researching Post-Compulsory Education*. London: Continuum.

Jones, C. (2005). *Assessment for Learning*. London: Learning and Skills Development Agency.

Kolb, D. (1984). *Experiential Learning*. Englewood Cliffs, NJ: Prentice-Hall.

Marton, F. and Saljo, R. (1997). 'Approaches to Learning', in F. Marton, D. Hounsell and J. Entwhistle (eds), *The Experience of Learning*. Edinburgh: Scottish Academic Press.

Maslow, A. (1954). *Motivation and Personality*. New York: Harper and Row.

Minton, D. (2005). *Teaching Skills in Further and Adult Education* (3rd edn). London: Thomson Learning.

Moon, J. (1999). *Learning Journals*. London: Kogan Page.

Moon, J. (2004). *A Handbook of Reflective and Experiential Learning: Theory and Practice*. London: Routledge Falmer.

Moser, C. (1999). *Improving Literacy and Numeracy: A fresh start*. London: DfEE.

Rogers, C. (1983). *Freedom to Learn for the '80s*. Columbus, Ohio: Merril.

Smith, A. (1996). *Accelerated Learning in the Classroom*. Stafford: Network Educational Press.

Smith, A. (1998). *Accelerated Learning in Practice*. Stafford: Network Educational Press

Stenhouse, L. (1975). *An Introduction to Curriculum Research and Development*. London: Heinemann.

Vygotsky, I. (1962). *Thought and Language*. Cambridge: MIT Press.

Vygotsky, L. (1978). *Mind in Society*. London: Harvard University Press.

Willis, P. (1999). 'Looking for What It's Really Like: phenomenology in reflective practice', in *Studies in Continuing Education*, 21, 1, pp. 91–112

Wood, M. (2001). 'Learning to Leap from a Peer: A research study on mentoring in a further and higher education institution', in *Research in Post-Compulsory Education,* 6(1), pp. 97–104.